Heroes of the Holocaust

2013142

Heroes of the Holocaust

By Susan Glick

LUCENT
BOOKS ®

THOMSON
TM
GALE

San Diego • Detroit • New York • San Francisco • Cleveland
New Haven, Conn. • Waterville, Maine • London • Munich

On Cover: (clockwise from center) Oskar Schindler, Vladka Meed, Hannah Senesh, Jan Karski.

LIBRARY OF CONGRESS CATALOGING-IN-PUBLICATION DATA

Glick, Susan.
    Heroes of the Holocaust / by Susan Glick.
       p. cm. — (History makers)
Summary: Profiles six individuals, some Jewish and some Gentile, who acted heroically in opposing the Nazi persecution of Jews in what came to be known as the Holocaust. Includes bibliographical references and index.
    ISBN 1-59018-063-1 (hardback : alk. paper)
    1. Righteous Gentiles in the Holocaust—Juvenile literature. 2. World War, 1939–1945—Jewish resistance—Juvenile literature. 3. World War, 1939–1945—Jews—Rescue—Juvenile literature. [1. Righteous Gentiles in the Holocaust. 2. World War, 1939–1945—Jewish resistance. 3. World War, 1939–1945—Jews—Rescue. 4. Holocaust, Jewish (1939–1945)] I. Title. II. Series.
    D804.65 .G55 2003
    940.53'18—dc21

                                    2002006978

CONTENTS

FOREWORD

The literary form most often referred to as "multiple biography" was perfected in the first century A.D. by Plutarch, a perceptive and talented moralist and historian who hailed from the small town of Chaeronea in central Greece. His most famous work, *Parallel Lives*, consists of a long series of biographies of noteworthy ancient Greek and Roman statesmen and military leaders. Frequently, Plutarch compares a famous Greek to a famous Roman, pointing out similarities in personality and achievements. These expertly constructed and very readable tracts provided later historians and others, including playwrights like Shakespeare, with priceless information about prominent ancient personages and also inspired new generations of writers to tackle the multiple biography genre.

The Lucent History Makers series proudly carries on the venerable tradition handed down from Plutarch. Each volume in the series consists of a set of five to eight biographies of important and influential historical figures who were linked together by a common factor. In *Rulers of Ancient Rome*, for example, all the figures were generals, consuls, or emperors of either the Roman Republic or Empire; while the subjects of *Fighters Against American Slavery*, though they lived in different places and times, all shared the same goal, namely the eradication of human servitude. Mindful that politicians and military leaders are not (and never have been) the only people who shape the course of history, the editors of the series have also included representatives from a wide range of endeavors, including scientists, artists, writers, philosophers, religious leaders, and sports figures.

Each book is intended to give a range of figures—some well known, others less known; some who made a great impact on history, others who made only a small impact. For instance, by making Columbus's initial voyage possible, Spain's Queen Isabella I, featured in *Women Leaders of Nations*, helped to open up the New World to exploration and exploitation by the European powers. Inarguably, therefore, she made a major contribution to a series of events that had momentous consequences for the entire world. By contrast, Catherine II, the eighteenth-century Russian queen, and Golda Meir, the modern Israeli prime minister, did not play roles of global impact; however, their policies and actions significantly influenced the historical development of both their own countries and their regional neighbors. Regardless of their relative importance in the greater historical scheme, all of the figures chronicled in the History Makers series made contributions to posterity; and their public achievements, as well as what is known about their private lives, are presented and evaluated in light of the most recent scholarship.

In addition, each volume in the series is documented and substantiated by a wide array of primary and secondary source quotations. The primary source quotes enliven the text by presenting eyewitness views of the times and culture in which each history maker lived; while the secondary source quotes, taken from the works of respected modern scholars, offer expert elaboration and/or critical commentary. Each quote is footnoted, demonstrating to the reader exactly where biographers find their information. The footnotes also provide the reader with the means of conducting additional research. Finally, to further guide and illuminate readers, each volume in the series features photographs, two bibliographies, and a comprehensive index.

The History Makers series provides both students engaged in research and more casual readers with informative, enlightening, and entertaining overviews of individuals from a variety of circumstances, professions, and backgrounds. No doubt all of them, whether loved or hated, benevolent or cruel, constructive or destructive, will remain endlessly fascinating to each new generation seeking to identify the forces that shaped their world.

The Importance of Heroes

The Holocaust was an event in World War II that is still difficult for many people to comprehend today. The Holocaust was the systematic destruction of 11 million people, 6 million of them Jews. This annihilation was ordered by Nazi dictator Adolf Hitler, who perceived of a powerful Third Reich, or third empire, made up of a master race of Germanic, or Aryan, people. He began his reign of terror in 1933 when he became chancellor of Germany and ended it in 1945 when he took his own life.

The Holocaust illustrates the worst qualities in humankind, but also the best. Villains abound, but so do heroes—heroes of all types.

It is important to remember the quiet heroism, the kind that occurred in private moments, witnessed by no one. The toddler who knew not to cry when the Gestapo pounded on the hiding-place wall. The woman who summoned her strength to hold up the person next to her so that neither would be selected for death. The father who saved his portion of bread for his son so that the child might eat. The mother who chose deportation to stay with her family. This is heroism—facing an incomprehensible evil with strength and courage.

Another kind of hero is the person who makes a conscious, deliberate decision to save the lives of others, often at the risk of his or her own life. There were many—though not enough—of this kind of hero in the war. These were often ordinary folks, both Gentile and Jewish, who found themselves facing a choice that required they listen to their inner voices, their own beliefs, and do what they believed was right, despite the enormous pressure—from their peers, from their government, even from their religious leaders—to do otherwise.

One such hero was Oskar Schindler, a man who, while not a saint, showed kindness to his factory workers throughout the war. Another is Raoul Wallenberg, a man who left the safety of Sweden to go to Hungary, where he saved thousands of people but lost his own life. Also, there was Vladka Meed, a young woman who saw her family taken in the Warsaw ghetto but continued to work as a smuggler for the underground, carrying messages, money, and weapons to further the resistance in Poland.

Other heroes include the French pastor André Trocmé, the spiritual leader of the village of Le Chambon, which hid thousands of Jews throughout the war; Zionist Hannah Senesh, who courageously left the safety of Palestine, dropped by parachute into Yugoslavia, and made her way back to her home country, Hungary, before she

A woman gives money to a boy. Acts of heroism as well as small acts of kindness occurred every day during the Holocaust.

was captured and shot; and the persistent Jan Karski, a witness to the Warsaw ghetto and one of the death camps, who tried to broadcast this story to the powerful Allied leaders.

These six people are among those who have been written about as heroes because, as Carol Rittner notes in the preface to *The Courage to Care,* these folks, and others like them, serve as a reminder "that to be human means to care about people who are in danger. They remind us that every person is responsible for his or her actions, and that each of us can make a difference." [1]

Schindler, Meed, Karski, Senesh, Wallenberg, Trocmé, and many others like them, had the courage of their convictions. They knew that what Hitler and the Nazis were espousing was wrong. And they each, in their own way, using their own individual talents and skills, took a stand.

Elie Wiesel, a Holocaust survivor and writer, speaks of what happens when people do not care, when there is indifference. Indifference leads to evil, he insists. The true heroes of the Holocaust were not indifferent. They cared about people, even people they did not know and had never met, people who in some cases were not like them, people whom they may have been encouraged to hate. "Let us not forget, after all," suggests Wiesel, "that there is always a moment when a moral choice is made. Often because of one story or one book or one person, we are able to make a different choice, a choice for humanity, for life. And so we must know these good people who helped Jews during the Holocaust. We must learn from them, and in gratitude and hope, we must remember them." [2]

CHAPTER 1

The Holocaust

When Adolf Hitler came into power in Germany in 1933, he brought with him a hatred for the Jewish people that would eventually result in the destruction of two-thirds of the Jews in Europe. By 1945, the year Hitler committed suicide, over 6 million Jews would be dead. This period of history, from 1933 to 1945, is referred to as the Holocaust, a word meaning "sacrifice by fire."

The 6 million Jews who died were victims of a genocide that was planned and carried out by the National Socialist German Workers' Party, or Nazis, under Hitler's direction. Another 5 million people were killed as well. Among those targeted were political prisoners, Jehovah's Witnesses, Roma (gypsies), homosexuals, and the mentally and physically handicapped who were part of Hitler's "euthanasia" program.

Although Hitler was a small, unimposing man, he was very charismatic. With the economy of Germany in a depression and unemployment high, it was not difficult for Hitler to persuade the German people that the Jews were responsible for these problems. Germany was a country with a long history of anti-Semitism, so when Hitler began restricting the rights of Jews in 1933, there was little opposition. In the twelve destructive years that followed, millions of innocent men, women, and children would be ruthlessly murdered.

Hitler's Rise to Power

Hitler's early life was not particularly remarkable. He was born in 1889 in Austria, and was raised by a doting mother and a strict, sometimes cruel, father who encouraged his son to pursue a career as a civil servant as he had. Hitler spent his early years on a small farm, and then moved several times between villages in Austria. When he was young, he was a good student who liked to read and draw. He dreamed of becoming an artist. His father, who scoffed at this idea, died when Hitler was fourteen. Several years later, Hitler dropped out of school and never returned to earn his high school diploma.

In 1907 at eighteen, he moved to Vienna where twice he submitted his work to the Academy of Fine Arts but was rejected both times. This angered him, and he refused to follow the academy's recommendation

Adolf Hitler (top row, far right) poses with his high school class at age fourteen. He was fourteen when his father died.

that he pursue architecture. Instead, he worked at odd jobs, lived on little money, and is remembered by acquaintances as being lazy and argumentative. In 1914, he joined the German army, fighting for four years on the front lines.

After World War I, Hitler's political life began to take shape. He became involved in the German Workers Party, a small, disorganized militant group with anti-Jewish sentiments. He began making speeches and producing propaganda, rising in power within this party, which he renamed the National Socialist German Workers Party (the Nazi party). In 1923, he participated in an attempt by the Nazis to overthrow the democratic German government and was arrested and jailed. While serving his brief prison term, he produced *Mein Kampf* ("My Struggle"). In it he presented his ideas about the blond-haired, blue-eyed Germanic master race and its enemy, the Jewish people.

After his release, Hitler continued his affiliation with the Nazis. A very effective speaker, he was able to persuade Germans that the Nazis could offer stability and jobs in the depressed economy brought on by the stock market crash in 1929. The Nazi party, led by Hitler, became the second largest party in Germany. In 1932, Hitler ran for the office of German president. He lost, but the elected president, Paul von Hindenberg, appointed him chancellor, the chief minister responsible for running the government, the following year.

As chancellor, forty-three-year-old Hitler surrounded himself with loyal, ambitious Nazis who would follow his commands and enforce his anti-Semitic policies. Hitler used the Nazi secret police, the Gestapo, and the security squad, the SS, also known as "black-shirts," to arrest and imprison anyone who opposed him. When President von Hindenberg died in 1934, Hitler became führer (the leader). He was now in complete control.

The Restriction of Rights

From his first days as chancellor, Hitler began restricting the rights of Jews. In 1933, Jewish-German businesses were boycotted; Jews were not allowed to attend cultural events; Jewish doctors and professors were ordered to leave their jobs. Anti-Semitic literature, including

Members of the SS pose with Hitler. Hitler liked to surround himself with men loyal to the Nazi party.

children's books, was widely published, presenting Jews as evil, untrustworthy, and sneaky. Books possessing what Hitler deemed "un-German" material—often by Jewish authors—were burned. In 1935, the Nuremberg Laws went even further. German Jews were no longer considered citizens of Germany. They were forbidden marriage with non-Jews and excluded from the military. Anyone who opposed such restrictions could be killed or sent to one of the German concentration camps, such as Dachau. Here prisoners were held in barracks, run through military drills, punished and tortured freely, and forced to work.

An Expanding Empire

While restricting the rights of the Jews, Hitler began rebuilding the German military. This action was in clear defiance of the Treaty of Versailles, an agreement Germany signed at the end of World War I in which it accepted responsibility for the war, promised to limit its troops, and promised not to engage in further military activity. In 1936, Hitler defiantly positioned lightly armed German troops in the demilitarized section of Germany known as the Rhineland. When neither France nor Britain responded, Hitler was elated.

In 1938, Hitler felt it was time to expand the German boundaries into Austria. He wanted more *lebensraum,* or living space, for the German people. Despite initial resistance on the part of the country's leaders, when the German troops entered Austria there was no military opposition. In fact, millions of Austrians were ethnic Germans and cheered this new affiliation. Again, no response came from France or Britain.

The next target for expansion would be Sudetenland, the northeast section of Czechoslovakia, home to 3 million ethnic Germans and an active pro-Nazi organization called the Sudeten German Party. This time Hitler negotiated an agreement with the leaders of Britain, Italy, and France, and Sudetenland was handed over without bloodshed.

In both of these countries, restrictions against Jews were immediately enforced. Jewish businesses and homes were looted. Jews were jailed for no reason, or forced to perform humiliating chores such as cleaning the streets or SS latrines. Many were run out of Austria and into Poland. Some were imprisoned in concentration camps in Germany.

Then, on November 9, 1938, a young Jew in Paris, Hershel Grynszpan, upset over the expulsion of his family from Germany, decided to do something to bring the world's attention to the plight of Germany's Jews. The seventeen-year-old Grynszpan entered the German embassy in Paris and shot a young German official, Ernst von Rath,

Germans pass by the broken shop window of a Jewish-owned business on the morning after Kristallnacht.

who later died. In retaliation, the Nazis lashed out in a night of destruction that some say marks the beginning of the Holocaust.

The Night of Broken Glass

Spurred on by the anti-Semitic campaign of propaganda minister Joseph Goebbels, the Nazis destroyed Jewish property all across Germany and Austria. In a destructive rampage, the Nazis set fire to synagogues, destroyed Jewish shops and homes, and killed over a hundred Jews. When this violent night was over, more than twenty thousand Jewish men were taken to concentration camps. This first pogrom, or massive attack against the Jews, was called *Kristallnacht,* or Night of Broken Glass.

Many Jews in Germany and Austria now realized the serious threat that the Nazis presented to them and knew they had to escape. Entire families left their homelands and attempted to gain entry into the United States, Palestine, Britain, and other countries. However, immigration quotas meant that people were turned away. Parents tried desperately to find safe places for their children, such as Kindertransport, a program that sheltered nine thousand German and Austrian children in Britain for the duration of the war. Jews who remained in Germany and Austria were eventually shipped out to ghettos or death camps.

A Turning Point in the Holocaust

The year 1939 marked a turning point. In March, Hitler's troops forcibly took the remaining provinces of Czechoslavakia. This angered the leaders of Britain and France, who now threatened to counterattack if German troops invaded Poland. Germany, seeking to reduce its enemies, signed a nonaggression pact with the Soviet Union in which they divided Poland and promised not to fight each other.

The German people did not want another war. They had suffered terribly in World War I, as had all of Europe. Hitler, however, was not to be stopped. On September 1, German troops entered Poland. The Allied powers of Britain and France declared war on Germany and World War II began. (The United States would follow in 1941 after Japan bombed Pearl Harbor.) Within a month, Germany captured Poland and the war against the Jews began in earnest. Jews were immediately segregated from the rest of society and stripped of rights.

The Ghettos

With millions of Jews in Greater Germany, the Nazis needed a way to contain them. After conquering Poland in 1939, the Nazis began to force the Jews in large cities into designated living areas called ghettos. A ghetto was a segregated section of the city, sometimes

Jews were forced to live in segregated areas called ghettos. Sometimes the ghettos were surrounded by barbed wire and high walls.

heavily guarded and sealed off with high walls. There were hundreds of ghettos in Eastern Europe, but nine major ghettos. The Warsaw ghetto was the largest.

When the Jews were forced into the ghettos, often at gunpoint, their possessions, homes, and businesses were seized. To further mark them as Jews, the SS required that they identify themselves with a special badge or band on the outside of their clothing, such as a yellow Star of David.

The living conditions in the larger ghettos were deplorable. Families were crowded into small living quarters, sometimes only a single unheated room. Water and food were scarce. Diseases, such as typhus and tuberculosis, were rampant. Often the bodies of the dead, many who had starved to death, lay unattended on the street.

To survive the ghetto experience, some Jews relied on food smuggled in and purchased on the black market. Sometimes people who had Aryan features, as did courier Vladka Meed, could cross outside of the ghetto walls and "pass" as non-Jews. In general, it was safer to be employed, often in the armament or supplies industries that supported Germany's war effort. This kept a person out of the path of the SS and also might earn them a larger ration of food.

The rules governing the ghettos were strict and often without reason. Ghetto inhabitants might be forbidden to sit on benches, use public transportation, or walk on a particular section of the sidewalk. Children were not allowed to be schooled. However, classes were held in secret, as were cultural events, such as music and theater performances. To control the Jewish people in the ghetto, the Nazis appointed a council of Jewish people, called *Judenrat,* to enforce Nazi demands. No one wanted to dispense orders given by the Nazis, but the *Judenrat* did, in some ways, contribute to order in the ghettos, such as by distributing food, running hospitals, and caring for orphans and the homeless.

Bold Advances

While this was occurring, Hitler continued to expand his empire, advancing now into Western Europe. In quick succession, German troops invaded Denmark, Holland, Belgium, Luxembourg, and France, leaving some of these countries with their own governments intact but under the authority of the Germans. In André Trocmé's country of France, for example, the Vichy government was a puppet of Germany.

The war took a dramatic turn in 1941 when Germany breached the German–Soviet nonaggression pact and invaded Russia. Three million Jews lived in Russia, and the German troops were under orders to kill as many as possible. Operating in special units known as *Einsatzgruppen*, Nazis rounded up and executed entire Jewish villages. One of the methods that the *Einsatzgruppen* employed was to kill Jewish people by cramming them in groups of fifty into airtight containers in the backs of mobile killing trucks and then piping in exhaust fumes from the truck engine.

Although precise numbers are not known, it is estimated that these *Einsatz* killings resulted in the death of as many as 2 million Russian Jews. This brutal operation was to last two years and would foreshadow the mass annihilation that would occur later in the war as the Nazis perfected their methods of systematized mass murder.

Camps

The Nazis also used camps to control their prisoners. Dachau was built right after Hitler came into power in 1933. Before the end of the war, there would be many more. Some were work or labor camps; others were extermination or death camps. Concentration camps served to hold people, sometimes for use as slave labor in nearby factories.

Living conditions at all the camps were brutal. In concentration camps, prisoners were forced to live in overcrowded, unheated barracks, where they slept four and five on the wooden slats of a bunk. Workdays might last up to fourteen hours and little food was provided. Anyone who showed any signs of resistance or was too weak to work would be shot. Many people died of starvation, exhaustion, and disease. By 1942, camps held over two hundred thousand prisoners. This number would more than triple within three years.

The "Final Solution"

Beginning in 1942, the camps would have an additional purpose: the mass slaughter of Jews. In January of that year, Reinhard Heydrich, the second in command of the SS, met with fifteen top commanders at a gathering called the Wannsee Conference. There the men discussed the "Jewish Problem." Incredibly, they came up with a plan to attempt to annihilate the 11 million Jews of Europe. Hitler called his plan the "Final Solution."

This barbaric plan could only be carried out with the systematic roundup and transport of millions of victims from the ghettos and work camps to six extermination camps located in Poland. That spring, the operation began. Train lines were full of victims being deported to death camps.

Jews in the ghettos were rounded up and told that they were being resettled for work purposes, and were asked to pack a few belong-

A German soldier prepares to shoot a Ukranian Jew on the edge of a mass grave. Mass burials were commonplace in Hitler's death camps.

ings to take with them. If they survived the grueling trip by train without food or water—and many did not—they arrived at camp, to be stripped, shaved, and sent into "showers" where poisonous gas would kill them. The bodies were then cremated or buried. To keep this horrific plan as secretive as possible, the Nazis had victims sign postcards and send them back home, assuring friends and relatives that they were well and working.

By the summer of 1942, the death camps were in full operation, with Jews from outlying countries such as Holland, France, Belgium, Norway, and Italy being brought directly to camps by train. In July 1942, Heinrich Himmler, head of the SS, ordered that "resettlement" be complete by December 31, 1942. In the month of August, over four hundred thousand Jews were deported and killed—or rounded up in ghettos and murdered as a group.

By now, reports of what was happening to the Jews of Europe were getting out to the rest of the world. The *New York Times* and the *London Daily Telegraph* both published articles in the summer of 1942 on what was happening. The World Jewish Congress also learned in that year of the Nazi plan to eliminate all Jews. Officials in the United States began to feel the pressure to respond, but little action was taken.

Resistance

Resistance groups, located in every ghetto, were learning the truth, as well. Underground leaders, such as the Jewish Fighting Organiza-

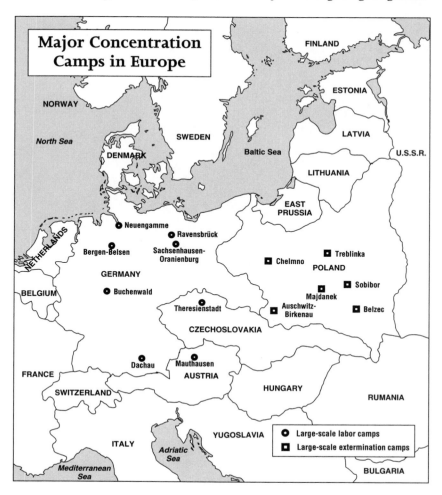

Jewish partisan fighters, such as the men seen here, lived Spartan lives in the forests of Germany.

tion in the Warsaw ghetto, began to persuade people that "resettlement" was a lie and that the death camps were murdering mass numbers of people. Underground groups were aided by Jewish partisans who lived a primitive life in forests throughout Eastern Europe. These partisan units, mostly made up of young people, had managed to escape from either ghettos, camps, or trains. They concentrated on thwarting the Nazis by sabotaging communications, blowing up railroad tracks and other key targets, obtaining weapons, or aiding couriers and others in hiding.

The most famous act of resistance was the Warsaw ghetto uprising. By early 1943, most of the people in the ghetto had already been deported. Only approximately sixty thousand of the original half-million ghetto inhabitants remained. Certain that death awaited them anyway, they decided to fight back. Underground fighters spent months gathering and building weapons and planning their counterattack. When the German troops entered on April 19, 1943, the first night of Passover, the fighters were ready with bricks, Molotov cocktails (homemade explosives in bottles), and grenades. The Germans were completely caught off guard. Fighting continued until May 16 when the Germans burned the ghetto to the ground. Some Jews were lucky enough to escape to the forests, but virtually all were killed. Other resistance efforts followed in other ghettos and camps, but nothing could match the force of the Nazis.

American soldiers view the bodies of prisoners who lay strewn on the grounds of a concentration camp. Liberators were shocked by the horrors they found.

Hungary Succumbs

The Nazis had a more powerful enemy to contend with—the Allied forces. In June 1944, British and American troops landed in Normandy and began pushing across Europe. Additionally, Soviet troops were moving into Poland, further forcing Germans into retreat. Germany was losing ground on all fronts.

Despite this, Hitler could not abandon his desire to rid Europe of Jews. In March 1944, German troops began deporting Jews from Hungary, a country that had sided with Germany earlier in the war but was now attempting to befriend the approaching Allies. Over four hundred thousand Hungarian Jews were quickly shipped to the death camp Auschwitz. When the railroad lines were no longer available, Jews were forced to march one hundred miles to Austria, but so many died on the way that marches were halted.

Instead, Jews remained in Budapest ghettos, prey to the violent Fascist group Arrow Cross, which murdered at random. Foreign diplomats, such as Raoul Wallenberg, struggled to save Hungarian Jews, but even so, by the time the Russians took over the city in February 1945, Budapest was destroyed and three-quarters of Hungary's Jews were dead.

Germany's Defeat

The Germans could not stop the Allied advance and they were forced to retreat. In the spring of 1945, the Russian and Allied troops reached the concentration camps from which the Germans had already fled. The liberators, as well as the rest of the world, were shocked at the horrors that were revealed when the camp gates were opened. Pits filled with decaying human remains, gas chambers that the Nazis were unable to destroy in time, cremation ovens still warm, and thousands of emaciated, dying prisoners revealed to the world the horror that had occurred. Many of the prisoners died even after they came under the care of their liberators. Many were simply too sick to recover. Others died from the rich food offered by well-meaning Americans and Russians. Some survivors were unable to even talk or to react, having suppressed their emotions for so long.

A Difficult Recovery

Survivors slowly made their way back to their native countries, searching for family members and friends. Many found that their countries still harbored deep feelings of anti-Semitism. Often homes and entire communities had been destroyed.

Relief organizations of the United Nations set up Displaced Person (DP) camps for survivors, and some people remained in them for years, too physically ill and mentally traumatized to resume an independent life. In time, however, despite limited immigration quotas, Jews began to relocate all over the world and begin again, often marrying fellow survivors. Palestine received the greatest number of immigrants, but survivors also moved to the United States, Argentina, Cuba, and Great Britain. In 1952, the final DP camp closed.

Few Nazis who were responsible for this atrocity were held accountable. Hitler himself committed suicide on April 30, 1945, as the Soviet army surrounded Berlin, just days before Germany surrendered on May 7. Other Nazis simply hid or were lost in the chaos following the war. When the Nuremberg trials were held in 1945, only twenty-two Nazi defendants were tried. In later years, more Nazis were located and brought to trial.

The story of the Holocaust is not over. Historians continue to uncover documents and make formal records and tape recordings of the personal narratives of survivors. The survivors themselves and their children still seek to make sense of what occurred. It is an event rich in lessons that the world is still learning. Key questions remain: How could this have happened? And what prevents it from happening again?

CHAPTER 2

Oskar Schindler: A Kind Nazi

With the popularity of Steven Spielberg's movie *Schindler's List,* Oskar Schindler may be the most recognized rescuer of the Holocaust. Protected by false pledges of loyalty to the Nazi regime and by countless bribes to those in power, Schindler was able to shelter more than a thousand Jews in factories where operations were staged to appear to be producing equipment for the war. In the beginning, Schindler was motivated by greed and used his Jewish workers to provide cheap slave labor in his factories. But he came to care about these people. Insisting that each of his workers was essential to the war effort, Schindler kept them warm and fed—and safe from the death camps where millions died. Schindler was that rare Nazi who was committed to saving lives, not taking them.

Childhood in a Small Mountain Town

In the perfect story of a hero, details from childhood would point to the heroic life that followed. However, Schindler's early life is not full of tales of special kindness or courage. In fact, his childhood was quite ordinary.

He was born April 28, 1908, in the town of Zwittau in what is now the Czech Republic. Zwittau was an industrial town, near the southern end of the Sudeten Mountains. The people who lived here, including the Schindlers, thought of themselves as ethnic Germans. They spoke German at home and in the schools.

The Schindlers lived a comfortable life in a big house, a villa with gardens around it. Oskar Schindler's father, Hans, owned a factory that sold farm equipment. Hans traveled a lot, leaving Oskar and his younger sister, Elfriede, at home with their mother. Oskar's relationship with his mother, Louisa, was close. Louisa was deeply religious, and some historians suggest that she gave Oskar the moral guidance that would later lead to his kindness toward the Jews.

Oskar's school years were unremarkable. In high school he studied engineering, math, and physics so that he might be better prepared to take over the family's factory. Schindler's interest in Jewish people and culture may have begun in his early years, in the neighborhood and at school. Among Schindler's Jewish classmates were the two sons of Rabbi Kantor. They lived next door and Oskar visited with them, the rabbi later said, to talk about Jewish literature and folktales, and ancient Jewish traditions.

As a teenager, Schindler showed some of the characteristics that he would later be known for as an adult. He liked excitement, especially fast cars and motorbikes, as did his father. He drove an unusual Italian motorcycle, a red 500cc Galloni, through the streets of his small town and participated in professional races with international racers on curvy mountain courses nearby. He liked winning and being the center of attention.

Marriage to a Farmer's Daughter

When he was twenty, Schindler married Emilie Pelzl, the daughter of farmers from the nearby village of Alt Moletein, also in the Sudeten Mountains. In the early years of their life together, Oskar and Emilie lived in Oskar's hometown, where he worked in his father's factory as a salesman. He traveled a lot while Emilie took care of Oskar's mother, whom she called Fanny, who was sick and confined to bed.

In her memoir, *Where Light and Shadow Meet,* Emilie Schindler describes her husband as a good man who could be difficult to live with. She writes, "In spite of his flaws, Oskar had a big heart and was always ready to help whoever was in need. He was affable, kind, extremely generous and charitable, but at the same time, not mature at all. He constantly lied and deceived me, and later returned feeling sorry, like a boy caught in mischief, asking to be forgiven one more time."[3]

Emilie shared with Oskar this concern for others in need, but she did not share Oskar's love of excitement. Emilie was an observant Catholic, like Schindler's mother, and had led a quiet, sheltered life, but Oskar liked to travel, attend

Oskar Schindler protected Jews from suffering in concentration camps by hiring them to work in his factories.

parties, and meet attractive women. He was known for his ability to consume large quantities of alcohol without appearing drunk or being ill the next day. He was also, according to his wife and others who knew him, very free with money. For example, Emilie says that after she and Oskar were married, Oskar, without her knowledge, took the large dowry given to them by her father and "bought a luxury car and squandered the rest on outings or unimportant things."[4] She found him wasteful and impulsive; he found her too frugal.

And yet these personality traits in Oskar Schindler were the same traits that later would enable him to arrange expensive, risky deals with his Nazi superiors during the war. His excessive drinking, womanizing, and spending made him a difficult husband, but he had a charm and magnetism that allowed him to convince people to give him what he wanted.

Involvement in the Nazi Regime

On January 30, 1933, when Oskar was twenty-five, Hitler came into power as the chancellor of Germany and began restricting the rights of Jewish people under German control. Schindler, who like others in the Sudeten region of Czechoslovakia identified himself as German, would join the Nazi party in 1939. He was not, nor would he ever be, a political man, but he did work as a spy for the foreign Nazi counterintelligence service, the *Abwehrdienst*. Schindler's job was to spy during his sales trips to Poland, identifying secret agents there. One of his assignments required him to obtain a Polish uniform so that the Germans could copy it and later infiltrate Poland in disguise.

Schindler enjoyed and was well suited for life as a double agent. He had a natural calmness to his demeanor and an ability to sit down with anyone, even people he despised, and over drinks get them to reveal what he needed to know. He also did not appear to fear the real risk involved. In 1938, the Czech government arrested him and condemned him to death, but charges were dropped when Germany invaded Czechoslovakia.

The reasons for his decision to spy for the Germans are not completely understood. Schindler may have wished to avoid further military service. He might also have been in agreement with the actions of the Germans against Poland and naive about the power Germany would come to exert over Czechoslovakia.

A Factory in Kraków

Germany's invasion of Poland the following year brought about big changes in Schindler's life. As did other entrepreneurs and industrialists, Schindler traveled to Poland's city of Kraków, looking for busi-

Nazis invade the Sudeten region of Czechoslovakia in 1939, the same year Schindler joined the Nazi party.

ness opportunities. In 1939, Schindler purchased the first of the two factories for which he would become famous. This first factory, at 4 Lipowa Street in Kraków, was a run-down enamel plant that Schindler renovated for production of pots and pans for the war. Schindler's contacts in the *Abwehrdienst* paid off, and he quickly acquired lucrative equipment contracts with the Germans. The factory, which he named the *Deutsche Emailwaren Fabrik,* or Emalia, was a successful enterprise for Schindler.

Schindler's factory relied on the cheap labor of Kraków's people. By the end of the first year, he employed 150 Jews, who were paid minimal wages. By the end of 1942, Schindler had almost 400 Jews, who arrived from the ghetto each day. However, these workers were no longer paid a wage. Instead, Schindler paid the SS a fee for each of his workers. Some historians and Holocaust survivors argue that Schindler was an opportunist who made millions from the cheap, forced labor the imprisoned Jews provided. Yet others, including those who worked there, insist that Schindler had real feelings for his workers, that he knew them all by name, and that he came to care

Schindler's factory was a safe haven for Jews during the Holocaust.

about them as people. And because of these genuine feelings of affection and friendship, he worked to make his factory a safe place, a haven from the overcrowded, dangerous ghetto. Ludmilla Page, an Emalia worker, insists that "people loved to work for him." [5]

Schindler, who had left Emilie back in Zwittau, was an impressive presence in the factory, standing more than six feet tall, with blue eyes and broad shoulders. He was a striking man and always impeccably dressed. Years later, survivors spoke of his warm, approachable personality and a friendly demeanor rarely seen in a Nazi. He is remembered for small things that he did; acts of kindness in a harsh world where beatings were common and workers could be shot on a whim. Many Emalia survivors tell of the extra food and medicines he provided and of his habit of dropping unfinished cigarettes on the ground, knowing that his workers would pick them up and finish them.

He bribed Nazi guards not to harm his workers, often dispensing bottles of vodka or schnapps to divert an intended punishment. He paid off SS inspectors who oversaw his operations, as well. With revenue generated from under-the-table sales of his enamelware, Schindler could strike deals with everyone. He traded diamonds, artwork, carpets, and vodka or cognac for favors. It was a corrupt system and everyone, from the highest officials on down, was part of it.

Isaac Stern, his Jewish bookkeeper throughout the war, describes how Schindler conned the inspectors:

> Almost every day, from morning until evening, "controls,"
> visitors and commissions came to the factory and made me

nervous. Schindler used to keep pouring them vodka and joking with them. When they left he would ask me in, close the door and then quietly tell me whatever they had come for. He used to tell them that he knew how to get work out of these Jews and that he wanted more brought in. That was how we managed to get in families and relatives all the time and save them from deportation. [6]

Protection from the Plaszow Labor Camp

With the Russians moving closer to the German front, life in the Kraków ghetto got worse. On March 13, 1943, Amon Goeth, commander of the nearby Plaszow labor camp, ordered the Kraków ghetto to be emptied, to be *judenrein,* "free of Jews." Schindler knew that life in the Plaszow labor camp was brutal. He had witnessed Commander Goeth's savage treatment of his prisoners. He had seen Goeth fire on innocent people at random, as if for sport. Infants, children, mothers, fathers, the very old—anyone could be shot, whipped, attacked by Goeth's dogs, or hung at any time.

Schindler wished to protect his workers from this terrifying commander. He came up with a plan to build barracks at Emalia and make it a subcamp. Schindler was able to convince Goeth and the other officials that his factory would be more productive if his workers lived on the premises. The camp included barracks, latrines, a camp laundry, a barbershop, and even a dental office.

SS guards oversee the deportation of Jews from the ghetto. Schindler saved lives by convincing Nazi officials to let some of the Jews work for him.

Once the workers were out of Plaszow, word spread further about the safety of Schindler's subcamp. Moshe Bejski, who lived there, remembers: "There was no killing whatsoever in the Schindler camp. In Plaszow hardly a day passed when there were no killings. Every German could kill at will. Schindler's people didn't work as hard as we worked in Plaszow. We worked fourteen to eighteen hours a day. Schindler provided supplementary food for his workers. An extra half a loaf of bread was very important in those times. . . . It was much desired to be transferred to the Schindler camp."[7]

The List

In August 1944, the political situation changed again. Schindler, who had been continually increasing his Jewish labor force, under new orders was forced to ship seven hundred of his workers back to Plaszow. Eager to save his remaining Jews, his *Schindlerjuden,* or his children as he referred to them, from certain death, Schindler came up with a plan to relocate his factory to Brinnlitz, in occupied Czechoslovakia, close to his hometown of Zwittau. Instead of producing enamelware, this new factory would produce shell cases for weaponry.

According to writer Herbert Steinhouse, one of the few to interview Schindler, to get permission to relocate his camp, Schindler "went to work on all his drinking companions, on his connections in the military and industrial circles in Kraków and in Warsaw. He bribed, he cajoled, he pleaded, working desperately against time and fighting what everyone assured him was a *Verlorene Sache*—a lost cause."[8] Finally someone with authority approved the move.

Former prisoner Leopold Page points out that Schindler went to great expense and trouble to gain approval for this move. He could have run away and hid until the war was over, insists Page. Instead, he stayed with his workers. "He spent the money. He saved us. He became a pauper. After the war, he didn't have a penny to his soul."[9]

Schindler began to draw up a list of names of those workers he wanted to transfer to his new factory. Everyone wished to be included. The list included the three hundred workers who remained at the factory and seven hundred to replace those who had been taken away, along with approximately one hundred additional names that were added to the list as it was being finalized. Schindler tried to include family members and other people he had made promises to, such as Helen Hirsch, who worked as a maid for Commander Goeth. Schindler had tried in the past to have Hirsch released from Goeth, who repeatedly beat her, but the cruel commander had refused. One evening, Schindler was able to win her freedom in a card game with a drunken Goeth. Her name, along with her sister's, was added to Schindler's list.

Four of Schindler's young Jewish workers take a break from their jobs. Schindler saved many Jewish children from the camps.

Everyone listed was given a trade, often fictitious, such as metalworker, machinist, or carpenter. Even children were presented as vital to the war effort. Later, when questioned, Schindler would make the absurd claim that children were essential because their small fingers could reach inside the shells to polish them.

"You Are with Me Now"

When the workers finally arrived at the Brinnlitz factory, Schindler greeted them in his famous Tyrolean hat. Ludmilla Page recalls him saying, "Don't worry, you are with me now." [10] After a long ordeal in the death camp Auschwitz before they got there, some of the women were too emaciated and ill to stand, let alone do any kind of work. So they were nursed back to health by Emilie Schindler, who had finally joined Oskar.

In addition to these original thousand or so, Schindler rescued others, including fugitives who had escaped from death camps. Late in the war, a train car of half-frozen, starving prisoners arrived at the factory, their bodies tangled in a frozen heap in the unheated compartment. Again, Emilie took care of the sick, and in an act of great significance to the prisoners of Brinnlitz, Schindler allowed the dead to be given a proper Jewish burial in a graveyard he had purchased for them.

Schindler spent enormous amounts of money to care for his *Schindlerjuden,* from his own accounts and through the sale of his wife's jewelry. Survivor Leopold Page estimates that the final eight months of the war cost Schindler 2 million prewar dollars.

The factory, Schindler's biggest deception yet, did not generate income. It was set up for protection of the workers, not for production. The Nazis believed that Schindler's factory was producing gun and tank shells, but in reality, it did not produce a single weapon used in the war. Quality control was deliberately low. And Schindler would fool officials by giving them munition products that had been produced elsewhere and purchased on the black market. On one occasion, his thirty-seventh birthday, he received notice that his shipment of shells had not been cast at the right temperature and could not be used. He was overjoyed, calling it the best birthday present he could have received.

Conditions at the work camp were harsh, but the acts of generosity by Schindler and his wife are legendary. Former prisoners tell of being allowed to sneak in oatmeal from a neighboring mill by filling the legs of their pants. Others relate how wool from a nearby abandoned mill was distributed among the workers so they could knit themselves warm socks and hats. Several survivors tell of the Schindlers providing them with new glasses after theirs had been broken or lost.

Brinnlitz Closes

In early 1945, Schindler knew the end of the war was near. Outside the camp, the Russians were advancing. On May 9, 1945, prisoners heard on their hidden BBC radio that the Germans had surrendered. In those final hours, Oskar called his workers together. He set up loudspeakers so that everyone could hear British prime minister Winston Churchill's announcement: "German armed forces surrendered unconditionally on May 7. Hostilities in Europe ended officially at midnight, May 8, 1945." Betty Sternlicht, who was there, describes the experience: "We could hear on the speakers that something was very exciting. We didn't understand, but we knew it was a voice of power, and Schindler let us listen. I realized this must be the end of the war. It was a feeling of, we are free! Goeth came to my mind right away: He can never come for me anymore." [11] The guards fled and the camp prisoners, still too disoriented to know what to do, stayed within the camp's walls for the next few days until they finally ventured into the nearby town in search of food.

In the following weeks, as the camp prisoners found their way back to what remained of their homes, they would remember Schindler's speech after the Churchill announcement. He begged them to remain human and not to seek revenge for all that they had lost. The courts and judges would seek justice, he had promised them. He gave each prisoner a bolt of fabric that he had stored for this day so that they could make themselves suitable clothes for travel, or use it for trade on the black market.

As the prisoners departed, a final goal remained: for both Emilie and Oskar Schindler to make it to safety. As the German owner of a slave-labor camp, Schindler had reason to fear for his life. The Russians could have easily mistaken him for a Nazi official and treated

Schindler (back row, center) reunites with some of the Jews he saved during the Holocaust.

him as a prisoner of war. His workers knew that and gave him a letter testifying to his aid during the war. They also gave him a ring on which they had inscribed the words "He who saves a single life saves the world entire." Several of them also chose to accompany the couple.

To disguise themselves, the Schindlers dressed in striped prisoner clothes. They traveled through the Czech countryside where German tanks burned in the fields and Russian troops shot Czech resisters. Afraid to be discovered as a Czech, Emilie discarded all the documents and memorabilia she had hastily packed. After several terrifying days, the Schindlers sought refuge with the Red Cross, who helped them board a train to neutral Switzerland where they would be safe.

During yearly visits to Israel, Schindler often met with Jewish children because they reminded him of the children he saved during the Holocaust.

After the War

In the years following the war, the Schindlers were unsettled. They lived in several German cities, relying on monthly care packages and financial donations gathered by Jewish families in the United States. Later, as Steinhouse relates, Polish welfare organizations offered assistance, but it was, in the end, the Jewish Joint Distribution Committee (JDC) that came to the Schindlers' assistance.

In 1949, the JDC raised funds to send Oskar and Emilie to Argentina. There, Schindler tried to make a living raising a minklike animal called a nutria. It was not the profitable fur business Oskar promised Emilie it would be, and in 1958, he left Argentina, leaving Emilie behind.

Alone and broke, Oskar Schindler returned to Germany. With more funds from the JDC, he opened a small cement factory, but this went bankrupt. According to Steinhouse, who interviewed Schindler around this time, Schindler "was hungry and depressed and living in a one-room place near the railroad station and still depending, in the 1960s, on handouts from the *Schindlerjuden.*" Steinhouse explains Schindler's struggles as a businessman: "He knew how to play the black market and he had known how to become a millionaire. Under wartime conditions of bribery and gifts he made money. But as a straightforward entrepreneur he apparently made a mess of things, in Argentina and again back in Germany." [12]

One highlight to this bleak existence were Schindler's yearly visits to Israel, beginning in 1962. Parties were thrown in his honor. He was loved by the Jews he had sheltered during the war because they recognized the risk he had taken. Explains former worker Leopold Page, "You have to have the guts to do something like this because the penalty for helping a Jew is a penalty of death, not only to the person, but his family, his whole village." [13]

When Schindler died in 1974 of heart and liver disease, he was only sixty-six years old. His funeral was held, according to his wishes, in a Catholic church in Israel. His *Schindlerjuden,* many of whom had never stepped into a church, came to honor him. "Almost all the mourners were Jews," [14] reports Steinhouse.

Recognition for Schindler

Before his death, Oskar Schindler was recognized for his humanitarianism as a non-Jew who aided Jews. In 1967, he was named "Righteous Gentile" by Yad Vashem, the Israeli authority for the Holocaust. And in 1993, almost twenty years after his death, Schindler was

The Medal of Remembrance was awarded to Schindler in 1993, nearly twenty years after his death.

awarded the rarely presented Medal of Remembrance from the United States Holocaust Museum. Schindler did not live to see himself become famous in Steven Spielberg's 1993 movie *Schindler's List.*

Schindler was once asked to explain what he had done in the war. He had this to say: "I hated the brutality, the sadism, and the insanity of Nazism. I just couldn't stand by and see people destroyed. I did what I could, what I had to do, what my conscience told me to do. That's all there is to it. Really, nothing more."[15]

CHAPTER 3

Raoul Wallenberg: A Man with a Mission

During World War II, Raoul Wallenberg made a choice. As a Swedish citizen, he could have safely waited for the war to end, watching from a distance as millions were murdered by Hitler. Instead, Wallenberg left the comfort of his neutral country and as a diplomat came to the dangerous city of Budapest, Hungary, where the Nazis were engaged in a desperate effort to kill as many Jews as possible before their forces fell to Russia and the Allies.

Wallenberg was an extraordinary diplomat. His unconventional methods of dealing with the Nazi bureaucracy succeeded in saving the lives of thousands of Jews. He distributed thousands of unique protective passes, set up safe houses, bribed officials, intercepted death marches, and thwarted a planned massacre of the Budapest ghetto. Tragically, Wallenberg was captured by the Russians before he could leave Hungary. His whereabouts since the day of his disappearance remain a mystery.

High Expectations

Raoul Wallenberg was born to a life of purpose and promise. The Wallenbergs of Sweden were a prominent family with a long history of accomplishment in the fields of banking, shipping, diplomacy, and military service. Andre Wallenberg, Raoul's great-grandfather a financial genius, founded the Stockholm Enskilda Bank, an institution that established itself worldwide.

Swedish diplomat Raoul Wallenberg used his diplomatic status to save the lives of many Jews.

Andre Wallenberg's sons continued this tradition of prominence and success, as did Raoul's father, Raoul Oskar Wallenberg, who was an officer in the Swedish navy.

Unfortunately, the elder Raoul Wallenberg died of cancer at the young age of twenty-three, four months before his namesake was born on August 4, 1912. The infant's young mother, Maj Wallenberg, took her son and went to live with her parents. Sadly, her own father, Raoul's maternal grandfather, died soon after. Six years later, Maj Wallenberg married a man named Frederik von Dardel, who treated Raoul like his own son. The marriage produced siblings for Raoul: a sister, Nina, and a brother, Guy.

Raoul Wallenberg was born into one of the most prominent families in Sweden.

Raoul was also guided early in his life by his paternal grandfather, Gustav Oskar Wallenberg, who had been an ambassador to Turkey and Japan. Gustav Wallenberg made it clear to the young Raoul that much was expected of him. In a 1929 letter, Raoul's grandfather took the opportunity to remind him, "When one comes from a family in which several generations have managed to acquire a certain reputation for competence and skill, it is more important than ever that you understand how unacceptable failure is as a legacy." [16]

Raoul did his best to live up to those high expectations. He was a serious child and an exceptional student. In some ways, he was different from the other children in his public school. Biographer Harvey Rosenfeld notes in *Raoul Wallenberg: Angel of Rescue* that while "classmates and friends occupied themselves with childlike games and interests, Raoul studied the financial progress of Sweden's large companies: at the age of nine, he was already collecting and reading the annual reports of those companies." [17] He was also interested at an early age in music, the Bible, and learning foreign languages. When he was fourteen, he journeyed alone on the Orient Express, a train that traveled across Eastern Europe to Constantinople (now known as Istanbul), where he met with his grandfather. Although Raoul was not a typical child, he was friendly and had a good sense of humor.

An American Education

After graduating high school in 1930, Raoul served nine months in the military. He then enrolled in a course in international studies in France. With his grandfather's guidance, Raoul chose to continue his education in the United States at the University of Michigan at Ann Arbor, where he studied architecture, and took advantage of vacations to travel all over the United States. Despite his family's prominence in Sweden, Raoul appeared to be an ordinary college student in Michigan. His classmate, Sol King, shares this memory:

> I still picture Raoul Wallenberg in gym shoes eating a hot dog—just a typical American college student. Neither his conduct nor his manner of dress gave any who knew him the slightest clue to his noble ancestry. In all that he did he managed to remain immensely unassuming. But one could not but realize the underlying brilliance. He was a modest person but a talented architecture student who showed great insight in finding simple solutions to complex problems. [18]

In 1935, Wallenberg graduated with a degree in science of architecture. He was awarded the Silver Medal of the American Institute of Architects for the graduate with the highest academic standing. Although ultimately he did not choose to stay with his art, when he returned to Sweden he worked briefly for an architectural firm. His first project was to redesign a public wharf. He enjoyed this project, but the young architect was still under the wing of his grandfather, who felt that banking had more of a future than architecture, particularly in the wartime recession that Europe was experiencing.

Palestine Connections

Relying on contacts made by his grandfather, Wallenberg left Sweden and traveled to Capetown, South Africa, where he worked briefly in marketing for a Swedish firm. After six months, he moved to Haifa, Palestine (now Israel), again using his grandfather's connections. While employed as an apprentice in a bank in Palestine, Wallenberg met many German Jews who had escaped from Nazi Germany. Wallenberg wrote home of his admiration for the Jews that he met here, commenting on the "boundless enthusiasm and idealism" of the

Zionists who had come there to establish a Jewish state in the dry, inhospitable desert where tensions between Arabs and Jews ran high. Wallenberg was impressed by their willingness to work so hard to settle in a "dry, stony little place surrounded by and already teeming with Arabs." [19]

At his boardinghouse, Wallenberg met German Jews who told him stories about how the Nazis had stripped them of their rights. Wallenberg not only developed a respect and affection for the Jewish people, he also thought of himself as someone with Jewish roots. His great-great-grandfather Michael Benedicks was a German Jew who immigrated to Sweden in 1780 and became a successful banker. After Benedicks married a Lutheran woman, he converted. Biographer Rosenfeld insists that "Raoul always considered himself a full Christian. But in 1936, as a compassionate, sensitive young man, the accounts of Jewish suffering in Germany had a profound impact on him." [20]

Travels Through Nazi Europe

When his apprenticeship ended, Wallenberg once again returned to Sweden. His devoted grandfather died in March 1937, and Raoul was without his grandfather's constant guidance and connections in the field of banking and business. In Stockholm, Wallenberg met Koloman Lauer, a Hungarian Jew who had an import-export business specializing in food and delicacies. Wallenberg began working as Lauer's international director. He traveled through Nazi-controlled Europe, learning as he went how to negotiate the Nazi bureaucracy. His work took him to Hungary, where he visited with Lauer's in-laws. Wallenberg grew increasingly concerned over the anti-Semitism of the Nazis.

Chosen for a Mission

Raoul Wallenberg's life was about to change completely. As an ally to Germany, Hungary's Jews had survived the war relatively unscathed. However, in March 1944, when Hungary's head of state refused to deport the Jews, Hitler sent in troops to carry it out. The Jewish Council of Hungary appealed to neutral countries for assistance. Norbert Masur of the World Jewish Congress contacted a chief rabbi in Stockholm, and a process began to find a suitable person to direct a rescue mission in Budapest. The United States' War Refuge Board, established in 1944 to rescue Jews and provide relief for victims of the war, got involved. Together with the Swedish Foreign Ministry, the War Board began looking for a man to direct this dangerous humanitarian mission in Budapest.

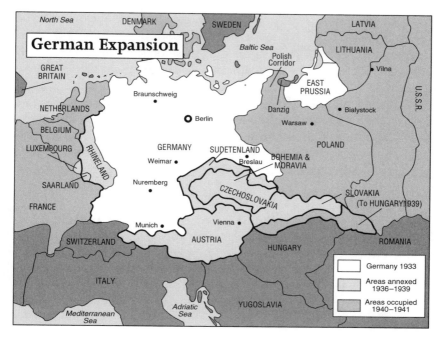

German Expansion

North Sea · DENMARK · SWEDEN · LATVIA
Baltic Sea · LITHUANIA
Polish Corridor
GREAT BRITAIN · Vilna
EAST PRUSSIA
Braunschweig
NETHERLANDS · Danzig · Bialystock · U.S.S.R.
O Berlin · Warsaw
BELGIUM
LUXEMBOURG · GERMANY · SUDETENLAND · POLAND
Weimar · Breslau · BOHEMIA & MORAVIA
SAARLAND · Nuremberg
CZECHOSLOVAKIA
FRANCE · SLOVAKIA (To HUNGARY 1939)
Munich · Vienna
SWITZERLAND · AUSTRIA
HUNGARY · ROMANIA
ITALY
Adriatic Sea · YUGOSLAVIA
Mediterranean Sea

Germany 1933
Areas annexed 1936–1939
Areas occupied 1940–1941

Raoul Wallenberg was chosen. Although he was young, only thirty-two, and had no experience as a diplomat, he had other qualities that made him suitable for the job of heading up the rescue mission. Per Anger, part of the overworked Swedish legation already in Budapest, agreed completely with this choice.

> I was convinced that no one was better qualified for the assignment than Wallenberg. He was a clever negotiator and organizer, unconventional, extraordinarily inventive, coolheaded, and something of a go-getter. Besides this, he was very good at languages and well grounded in Hungarian affairs. At heart, he was a great idealist and a warm human being.[21]

When told of the dangers of the mission, Wallenberg was undaunted. He was eager to save even a single person in need.

Arrival in Budapest

On July 9, 1944, Wallenberg arrived in Budapest. He carried with him a letter from the Swedish king, Gustav V, to Hungarian regent Miklos Horthy, and a list of the names of Jews who might be in danger in Hungary. He also had with him a list of people who might help him: secret agents and other anti-Nazis in government positions. Immediately, Wallenberg began contacting these people, establishing the connections he would come to rely on during the course of his rescue mission.

From those informants, Wallenberg gathered the information he needed to begin sending home a series of reports called "Memorandum Concerning the Jews of Hungary." In these detailed dispatches, Wallenberg delivered the brutal truth about such things as the inhumane conditions in the camps, the deportation trains, and the current situation for the Jews of Budapest by the summer of 1944. While Hungary's regent Miklos Horthy had halted the deportations begun in March, over four hundred thousand men, women, and children had already been transported to the death camps. When Wallenberg arrived in July, only two hundred thousand Jews were left in Budapest.

Newly Designed Protective Passes

Wallenberg needed to work fast in order to help the remaining Jews. Quickly, he assembled a staff of Jewish volunteers to assist with his rescue efforts. His staff, which grew to include over four hundred Jews and their families, was granted diplomatic protection as employees of a neutral legation. This meant that they were exempted from wearing the yellow star identifying them as Jews and could not be forced out of their homes.

Thousands of Hungarian Jews received passes like this one thanks to Wallenberg's efforts.

With the help of this staff, Wallenberg greatly expanded the program of issuing protective passes or Swedish passports, which were given to Jews who had connections with Sweden. One of the first things Wallenberg did was to redesign and reissue Swedish protective passes. Knowing that the Germans would be impressed with a more formal document, Wallenberg, using funds supplied by the United States, replaced the ordinary-looking passes with something far more elaborate. John Bierman, author of *Righteous Gentile,* describes the Wallenberg pass:

> Here his architect's training in design and draughtsmanship came into play, and the Wallenberg passport was a stroke of genius. He had it printed in yellow and blue, embellished with the triple crown of the

Swedish government, and dotted with seals, stamps, signatures, and counter-signatures. Though it had absolutely no validity in international law, it inspired respect, serving notice to the Germans and Hungarians that the holder was not an abandoned outcast but under the protection of the leading neutral power of Europe. These passports also gave a big boost to the morale of those Jews who received them.[22]

The passes allowed Hungarian Jews the right to be recognized as Swedish citizens, including, although such travel was not possible, the right to travel to Sweden. Most important, the holders of the pass were protected from deportation. The young diplomat met with Regent Horthy and got permission to issue five thousand of these passes. In actuality, Wallenberg issued far more than the agreed-upon number. Some diplomats feared that the city would be flooded with too many passes, but the success of his passes inspired other neutral countries such as Portugal, Switzerland, and Spain to step up their own rescue efforts. An estimated fifty thousand Jews were saved as a result of these passes.

Support for the City's Jews

During this same time, Wallenberg worked feverishly to support the city's Jews in other significant ways. He quickly began to set up "safe houses" or "Swedish houses" under protection of the Swedish flag. The safe houses were apartments and houses Wallenberg found and rented in Pest, the Jewish section of the city. Those with protective passes would live here and be supplied with food, clothes, and medicines as needed. This was an enormous undertaking, and the homes grew overcrowded with Jews seeking refuge. Other neutral diplomats, such as those from Switzerland and Portugal, followed suit and by the end of the year, over thirty thousand people were sheltered in these protected houses.

Wallenberg, with the International Red Cross, also set up two fully staffed hospitals, one of them specializing in the infectious diseases that were rampant as living conditions deteriorated. Protected Jews and Wallenberg's staff were inoculated against typhoid and cholera. The hospitals were full and at overcapacity. Wallenberg also set up programs for children and the elderly in the safe houses.

Reign of Terror Returns

In August 1944, Regent Horthy fired his pro-German prime minister, a move resulting in part from the pressure exerted by Wallenberg and other diplomats. With the German presence lifted, life for Budapest Jews improved. The Russians were advancing and the end of

Ferenc Szalasi (right), leader of the Arrow Cross, attempted to prevent the use of protective passes.

the war seemed to be in sight. Wallenberg, feeling that his work was done, made plans to return home before the Russian troops entered the city.

Such optimism was unfounded. On October 15, 1944, the Germans rose up, overthrew the Horthy government, and replaced it with one led by Ferenc Szalasi, leader of the Nyilas, or Arrow Cross, organization. The Arrow Cross, along with the return of SS Lt. Colonel Adolf Eichmann, brought the Jews of Budapest into a savage period of destruction unparalleled in Hungarian history.

Elenore Lester, author of *Wallenberg: The Man in the Iron Web*, writes: "Jews who dared to leave their homes were murdered; their unburied bodies littered the streets of the city. In the meantime, the Szalasi gangs went from home to home, looting, flogging, and selecting victims for deportation."[23] Wallenberg, thrown back into his work, organized young Jews in commando units to bravely enter the ghetto, taking food and medicine to those who were imprisoned in their homes.

The Szalasi government also revoked the use of protective passes. Ever resourceful, Wallenberg used his friendship with Elizabeth Kemeny, the wife of the foreign minister, to exert pressure on the new regime to restore the use of protective passes, as well as other basic rights that had been taken away from Jews. To save time, Wallenberg simplified his pass, making it a less elaborate single-page document.

Death Marches Begin

The situation in Budapest worsened considerably with new orders from Eichmann. In a frantic attempt to empty the city of Jews before the Russians entered it, Eichmann issued orders to continue with deportation. The railway lines to Auschwitz had been bombed by Allied troops, so the victims were forced to march across the country to a death camp on the Austrian border. Beginning on November 20, 1944, and lasting for five weeks, Jews were grabbed off the streets and forced to march over a hundred miles. Without food or warm clothes in the freezing air, as many as ten thousand died along the way before these marches were stopped.

Wallenberg rushed to intercept the marches and then later the trains, showing up with protective passes at assembly centers to persuade the German officials to release people. Fellow Swede Per Anger remembers how Wallenberg would arrive and quickly pull out a number of desperate Jews who had "no passport at all, only various papers in the Hungarian language—drivers licenses, vaccination records, or tax receipts—that the Germans did not understand." Wallenberg would insist that these prisoners were under his protection and the Germans would let them go. According to Anger, "The bluff succeeded." [24]

Fermec Frieman remembers being saved by Wallenberg after she was forced out of one of the Swedish safe houses. The train to the death camp was to arrive at any minute, but suddenly two cars pulled up. According to Frieman "There was Wallenberg in the first one, with Hungarian officials and German officers in the second car. He jumped out, shouting that all those with Swedish papers were under his protection. I was one out of the 150 saved that day. None of the others ever came back." [25]

Susan Tabor is another survivor who remembers Wallenberg for promises made and kept. She was taken with thousands of others to a brick factory outside Budapest. She was held there with no food, no water, and no bathrooms. Wallenberg came, saw what was happening, and promised to try and return. Says Tabor, "He also said that he would try to get medical attention and sanitation facilities. And true to his word, soon afterward some doctors and nurses came from the Jewish hospital. But what stands out most about Raoul Wallenberg is that he came himself. He talked to us, and most important, he showed that there was a human being who cared about us." [26]

In his desperate efforts to save as many people as possible, Wallenberg relied on unconventional methods. He used his contacts in the government to make bribes for delays or even to stop a march. Not afraid to be bold, Wallenberg had his Jewish staff disguise themselves in Arrow Cross uniforms and enter camps and prisons, claiming that they had orders to take certain Jewish prisoners for deportation.

Raoul Wallenberg's actions put him in danger. He was hated by the Arrow Cross. And according to Per Anger, they wanted to kill him. However, Wallenberg was not intimidated, and rather than seek safety, he instead moved his offices to the Pest section of Budapest where the two Jewish ghettos were located.

During the month of December, the Arrow Cross kept up its barbaric crusade against the Jews. A report filed by the Institute of Forensic Medicine in Budapest describes their horrible deeds:

> In the most brutal manner, the Nyilas made short work of their victims. A few were simply shot, but the majority were mercilessly tortured. From the distorted faces of the corpses the conclusion could be drawn that their sufferings had been ghastly. . . . Shooting out of eyes, scalping, deliberate breaking of bones, and abdominal knife wounds were Nyilas specialities. [27]

Saving the Central Ghetto

In what would be his final heroic act, Wallenberg was able to stop the planned massacre of all sixty thousand Jews in the central ghetto. Through a contact Wallenberg had established with an Arrow Cross official named Pal Szalay, Wallenberg was able to threaten that if the massacre occurred, he would see to it that August Shmidthuber, commander in chief of troops in Hungary, would be held accountable for this war crime. With the Russians near to the city and Germany's fall imminent, Shmidthuber was persuaded that Wallenberg was right and that he would hang for this crime. The order for the massacre was rescinded. When the Russians entered the city in January 1945, the ninety-seven thousand Jews who lived in the city's two ghettos were still alive, thanks in great part to Wallenberg and his extraordinary accomplishments.

Wallenberg Disappears

Although Wallenberg had saved a number of lives, his work was not done. He was still interested in the welfare of the Hungarian Jews, having in mind a final program to aid those who had lost their families,

An extended Jewish family hidden by Wallenberg in Budapest's central ghetto.

their jobs, and their property in the war. He called this plan the "Wallenberg Institute for Support and Reconstruction" and was eager to speak with both Hungarian and Russian officials about it.

On January 17, 1945, Wallenberg was called to the Russian headquarters in Debrecen, east of Budapest. He and a driver were accompanied by Russian soldiers. Before he departed, Wallenberg told a friend, apparently in a joking manner, that he was not sure whether he was going as a guest of the Russians or a prisoner. Wallenberg and his driver never arrived at Debrecen. It is believed that they were taken to Moscow and put in prison.

For a long time, the Russians denied knowledge of Wallenberg's whereabouts, but finally on February 6, 1957, they announced that Raoul Wallenberg had died in his Russian prison cell of a heart attack on July 17, 1947, and that his remains had been cremated. This report was doubted by many. It conflicted with earlier reports by the Russians and was disputed by prisoners who claimed to have seen Wallenberg in person. Some reports have him alive in Soviet prisons as late as the 1950s. There has been some speculation that the Russians thought he was an American spy. His sympathy for the Jews made him suspect.

Many people believe that Sweden could have been more aggressive about demanding the release of Wallenberg, particularly in the early years. Other political prisoners were freed by negotiating the trading of prisoners, for example. It is argued that Sweden's officials were too timid, too interested in avoiding confrontation with Russia. Later, when pressure was exerted on the Soviet Union, it was too late. Throughout the long years of Wallenberg's disappearance, his parents, who died in February 1979, held out hope that their son would be returned home.

Honors Bestowed

Raoul Wallenberg never received the honors awarded him for his service and heroism in Hungary. By some estimates, he is responsible for saving the lives of one hundred thousand Jews. Three countries

A commemorative U.S. postage stamp honoring Raoul Wallenberg is just one of many tributes to the Swedish diplomat.

have granted him the extraordinary distinction of honorary citizenship: the United States (1981), Canada (1985), and Israel (1986). Wallenberg is recognized as one of the Righteous Among Nations in Israel, and countless streets and buildings in various countries honor him by carrying his name.

Raoul Wallenberg's extraordinary achievements will be remembered forever. His remarkable accomplishments in Budapest are a source of inspiration and a reminder to all that the impossible can be achieved when even a single man takes a determined stand against evil.

CHAPTER 4

Vladka Meed: Between Two Worlds

When Vladka Meed, born Feigele Peltel, joined her first youth group as a young Jewish girl, she could not have imagined the life that lay ahead of her. After the Germans invaded Poland, her family was forced to live in the Warsaw ghetto. Her father died and her mother and siblings were deported. Alone in a city at war, Vladka's new family became her comrades in the youth organizations of the Warsaw underground.

Vladka Meed, passing as a Polish Gentile, became a smuggler for the resistance movement. Her mission was to smuggle weapons and information into the ghetto in preparation for the Warsaw ghetto uprising. It was risky work and many in the resistance died, but Vladka was able to avoid capture and survive a war that took all of her family and many of her friends.

Her involvement in the underground took many forms, including the rescue of children for whom she found hiding places with Polish Christians. She also established contact for partisan fighters in the woods and the labor camps, smuggling in information, food, and other supplies. Her support for Jews didn't stop with the end of the war. She continues to this day to work in the field of education, directing yearly seminars for teachers about the Holocaust.

Jewish Childhood in Warsaw

Vladka Meed's life started out quite ordinary. She was born in 1923 in Warsaw, Poland, to Shlomo and Hanna Peltel and lived in a small apartment with her sister, Henia, who was younger by two years, and her brother, Chaim, who was six years younger. Vladka's father was a leather factory worker and her mother owned a small haberdashery business. Shlomo Meed was a scholarly man who liked to read, Vladka recalls in an extensive oral history interview that she gave in 1991.

Vladka Meed, then Feigele Peltel, lived in a traditional Jewish home, although it was not particularly religious. Her father insisted she attend a Yiddish secular school sponsored by the Jewish Socialist Bund, a prominent political group in Warsaw that worked to support the rights of the Jewish people. From the age of ten, Vladka was a member of the Bund. According to Vladka, this connection with this political organization would continue throughout her life, "like a chain from the beginning of my childhood." [28]

When the Germans occupied Poland in 1939, her father assured the family that despite the hard conditions being imposed on them, the German soldiers would treat them fairly. That had been his experience from World War I, and he believed it would prove true again. It did not. Her father was thrown from the breadlines because he was Jewish, and the family was unable to obtain the food they needed. Vladka, whose blue eyes, small nose, and light hair enabled her to pass for a Gentile, was able to remove her armband and to support her family by both standing in breadlines and traveling to the rich sections of Warsaw to sell merchandise from her mother's shop. Sometimes her sister and mother would accompany her, stand at a distance, and warn her if the Germans were approaching. "In the beginning I was afraid," she recalls, but she considered it a challenge. "It felt good" and "important" [29] to be helping her family.

The Move to the Ghetto

When the Jewish people were moved to the ghetto in the fall of 1940, the situation became more desperate. The family lived in shabby living quarters consisting of only a kitchen and a single bedroom. Meed recalls how the walls were wet with dampness. In this unhealthy environment, her father got pneumonia. According to Meed, with food scarce, "we weren't able to feed him the right food." [30] Her father never recovered, and died.

Life in the ghetto was difficult for everyone who lived there, and anti-Nazi, pro-Jewish underground groups, such as the Bund, the Zionists, and the Jewish Fighting Organization (ZOB), were active. These groups gathered information from outside the ghetto about what was happening throughout Poland and the rest of Europe.

Vladka Meed changed her name and identity in order to smuggle Jews out of Poland.

They disseminated this information through pamphlets and newsletters. Meed distributed some of these materials, including the Bund magazine. This was a dangerous form of resistance, but in the Warsaw ghetto it was the young people who were the first to embrace an organized response to the Nazis.

Meed and her young friends met in small groups to hold lectures and meetings. In these early days, her mother was happy to see her involved in something. Despite the many hardships of the ghetto, her family, now without a father, tried to carry on a normal life. For example, although food was limited, her mother still managed to hide bread to pay the rabbi for bar mitzvah training for Vladka's brother. However, Vladka knew that her activities in the underground put her at risk of arrest. To protect her family, she moved to another apartment not far away.

Her Family Deported

Meed had been living in the ghetto for two years when deportations began. With little warning the Germans rounded up hundreds, sometimes thousands, of Jews and transported them out of the ghetto to an unknown destination. In her memoirs, *On Both Sides of the Wall,* Meed describes the day her life changed irrevocably. It was July 22, 1942. "Like the rest of us," Meed writes, "my mother assumed that the approaching deportations were merely transfers to some other region. After all, for months now the ghetto had been filled with trucks and horse-drawn wagons, bringing Jews from nearby towns. Now, we imagined, it would be our turn to be moved to another place." [31]

Vladka's mother and fifteen-year-old brother were deported to the camp called Treblinka, leaving her sister and her behind. A neighbor was able to escape from the *Umschlagplatz,* the deportation site, and give Vladka a scribbled note from her brother. Vladka describes this final message: "They were lining up for their bread ration, Chaim had written. They were unendurably hungry and thirsty and had better hurry, lest the food run out and they would be thrust into the railroad cars without a crumb to eat. That was all . . . and they were the last words to reach me from my mother and my brother." [32] Then, not long after this, her sister, Henia, was deported as well. The loss of her entire family left Vladka bereft.

Numb with grief, she found work as a seamstress, a skill her mother had once encouraged her to learn. The work was hard and there was no food. The shifts sometimes lasted thirty hours, but it was safer to be working because those not employed were far more vulnerable for a roundup. As Meed recalls in her memoirs, "Time

SS guards corral Jews for deportation to a concentration camp after a ghetto uprising.

dragged. The sewing machines clattered unceasingly. Heads heavy, tongues parched, eyes burning, we saw nothing but green cloth, guided under the needle, ten centimeters for the width, ten centimeters for the length. Squares upon squares, and these into larger squares—a universe of squares—squares, our only horizon." [33]

Joining the Resistance

As the deportations continued, resistance leader Abrasha Blum announced the formation of the Jewish Coordinating Committee that would work to coordinate the various underground groups. These groups, such as the Zionists and the Bund, believed in a different set of principles for the future of Jews, but now, in the ghetto, they were united in their resistance to the Nazis.

Blum recognized Meed's Aryan features and made her an offer. He asked her if she would support the movement by passing out of the ghetto and working for the resistance from the Aryan side. Meed agreed. Without her family, she had nothing to lose. "This was the high point of my remaining in the ghetto after the family was taken," Meed admits. "It was not the feeling of being afraid. It was just the opposite. It was the feeling . . . that I can do something, a challenge for which I was eager to take." [34]

Crossing Over

On December 5, 1942, she crossed out of the ghetto for the first time. It was almost a disaster. Carrying in her shoes an underground bulletin that contained drawings and a description of the Treblinka death camp, she joined the line of workers who left the ghetto each day. Suddenly she was called to the side and detained. Taken into a shack for interrogation, she was told to remove her shoes. She knew that if she did so, the underground documents would be found and she would be beaten or killed. Fortunately, the attention of the guard was momentarily diverted and she ran from the shack and succeeded in passing out of the ghetto.

On the other side, she discarded her armband and proceeded to walk the streets as though she belonged there as a Polish girl, not a Jew. She found she could easily pass as a Gentile with her Polish features. She also had a certain way of carrying herself, a manner of keeping her emotions in check.

As she moved through Warsaw, she was stunned to find that life in the Aryan sector was untouched by the death and destruction occurring in the ghetto: "Here it was as if nothing had happened in the last two years. Trolleys, automobiles, bicycles raced along; businesses were open; children headed for school; women carried fresh bread and other provisions. The contrast with the ghetto was startling. It was another world, a world teeming with life." [35]

Meed located her underground contacts in the Aryan sector. With their help, she was able to acquire false papers that identified her as a Polish Gentile, to secure safe housing, and, with the help of a Polish woman named Wanda Wnorowska, to obtain a job as a seamstress. Not long after her new life as an Aryan was established, Vladka began meeting secretly with various leaders of the underground groups.

A Turning Point

Her first meeting was arranged by friend and Bund activist Michal Klepfisz and held in what was a typical gathering place for the underground, a public kitchen or cafeteria. Michal's contact was a prominent Bund representative on the Aryan side, Mikolai Berezowski. In her memoir, *On Both Sides of the Wall,* Meed describes how Berezowski asked her to join the force of volunteers who were needed to make contact with Gentiles and find new hiding places, particularly for women and children. He also asked her if she would smuggle weapons into the ghetto. Both these jobs were dangerous work. He warned her that "we must be very careful; if we make one mistake, we can get a lot of people into very bad trouble." [36]

The work would be unlike anything Meed had ever done. It would require courage, along with ingenuity and resourcefulness. Berezowski told her, "As far as possible, each of us must create his own tasks; that is, try to cultivate new friendships, but he must do so with the utmost caution." [37]

Vladka agreed to participate in these vital—and dangerous—activities of the underground. Later she would refer to this discussion as "a turning-point in my life and activities." [38]

Meed began her work as a smuggler. She made her own contacts in the Gentile world and searched endlessly for Polish families who would agree to shelter Jews, particularly children. As the deportations increased, this was increasingly a goal of the underground. Meed would later write, "We spared neither effort nor expense in trying to persuade Poles to hide Jewish children in their homes." [39] Sometimes parents in the ghetto refused to give up their children, even when a safe alternative had been found, preferring instead to keep the family together. But many children survived the war by being placed with Polish families who put themselves at great risk of death if discovered.

Meed's work was dangerous. Warsaw was a corrupt city, full of Polish informants. If an informer suspected her of being Jewish, the informant could either turn her in to the authorities, or, as was common, threaten to turn her in unless a bribe was paid. Bribery was rampant in the city of Warsaw and informants demanded outrageous payment for silence. Meed called what they did "diabolical work." She describes what it was like to live under this constant threat of betrayal: "Our rooms were always filled with underground

Meed worked as a courier in the Jewish underground movement.

55

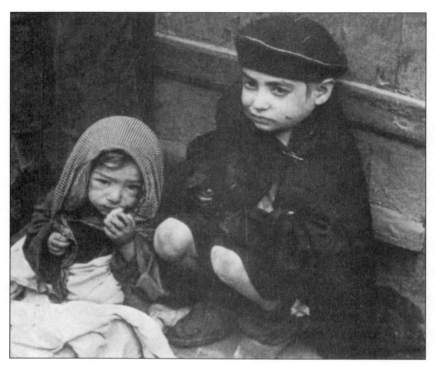

Meed found Polish homes for Jewish children orphaned during the Holocaust.

leaflets, notices, and forged documents. We kept most of them in my bed out of sight of our landlady. We lived in constant fear. We had reason to believe that the informer in our midst, whoever he might be, was continuing his work. We changed our addresses and identity cards with utmost secrecy. We avoided Stephan [a suspected informant]. Every evening we met, our faces reflecting our inner anxiety: What new misfortune had befallen us today?" [40]

The January Resistance

On January 18, 1943, a change occurred in the Warsaw ghetto. This time, when the deportations began, the Jews chose to hide. When they were found, they surprised the Germans with their first organized resistance, led by Mordecai Anilewicz of the Jewish Fighting Organization. The fight was effective, but the resisters, without ample weapons, were quickly subdued. However, this first act of defiance marked a change in the mood of the ghetto. It indicated that people were becoming more desperate. They were starting to believe what the underground groups had been telling them: the death camps were real. Many people began to accept resistance as their only hope. "Don't let yourself be taken away. This was the motto of the ghetto at this time,"[41] Meed recalls.

Meed and other smugglers hurried to bring in dynamite and as many guns as they could find. "All of us," writes Meed, "sensed the final, decisive moment was at hand."[42]

The Loss of Friends and Comrades

Vladka entered the ghetto one final time to bring in explosives. She could see preparations being made for the Warsaw uprising that was to come. She saw posters boldly inviting resistance; individuals who were arming themselves; a factory secretly producing German uniforms. She left the ghetto and returned to the Aryan side.

On April 19, 1943, the Warsaw ghetto uprising began. Meed watched in anguish from the Aryan side. From a vantage point close to the wall, she witnessed the ghetto burning and knew that people were dying. She describes her feelings at the time:

> With their pitiful assortment of arms and explosive-filled bottles our comrades in the ghetto had dared to challenge the modern, sophisticated weapons of the enemy. We on the "Aryan side" were bursting with admiration for them, but we were consumed by a sense of guilt at being outside the ghetto, in relative safety, while they were fighting and dying. We should have been there with them, amid the roaring fires and the crashing walls.
>
> We stared into the fiery sky over Warsaw. Why was there no response from the rest of the city? Where was the help our neighbors had promised? And the rest of the world—why was it so silent?[43]

The Warsaw ghetto was destroyed. Most of her friends and comrades were dead. Less than a hundred people had managed to escape and were hiding in the woods with the partisan fighters. Meed felt that her life was finished. She was angry at herself for not being there and terribly lonely now, without her comrades. The underground fighters who had perished had become her family. Some she had known since childhood. "I was absolutely a piece of pain,"[44] she later recalled in an interview.

Before Meed left the city of Warsaw, one final tragic event occurred. Resistance leader Abrasha Blum, who had survived the uprising from the Aryan side, sought shelter with her, hiding in her closet. However, he was discovered and they were both arrested. Fortunately, Vladka was able to send a note to a Polish woman who had helped her repeatedly in the past and who now secured a bribe for her release. Blum was not so lucky. He was taken to the Gestapo and killed before anything could be done.

Away from Warsaw and Alone

After being released, Meed left Warsaw and spent time in the countryside, living life as a Gentile. It was a time of isolation for her, one in which she was free to think about all she had lost in the war. She recalls that time period:

> My mind filled with memories, visions—of my parents, my sister, my brother, my friends, my relatives, my comrades. In my imagination, I returned to the turbulent world I had known before. I heard their loud voices, my mother puttering about the kitchen. I saw her wrinkled, emaciated face, her keen brown eyes, the swollen blotches left by hunger. She seemed to be smiling. Yes, she could be at ease now—I was no longer starving, and now I could get enough bread for her too. The swelling on her face would soon vanish, if only she could have stayed with me a while longer. But her face receded and harsh reality returned to engulf me with its full force. [45]

After a month or so of hiding, Meed returned to Warsaw and continued her work as a smuggler, finding hiding places for refugees, and carrying money, forged documents, and information to those in hiding. The goods and information were sent via the Coordinating Committee and other relief organizations such as the Bund and the Relief Council for Jews. This was dangerous work but necessary to help the thousands of refugees. Vladka also smuggled letters and money into German labor camps. Prisoners were able to bribe guards for more food and medicine, particularly for children.

What she calls the only bright side in her sad life at this time was her friendship with a man named Benjamin Miedzyrzecki (later Benjamin Meed), the man who would become her husband after the war. She spent time with him and his family, who were in hiding. They were able to carry on a courtship that sometimes felt normal. Benjamin, like Vladka, had Aryan features, so they could move somewhat freely about Warsaw.

Liberation and Emptiness

In the final months of the war, Vladka and Benjamin left Warsaw, passing through Poland as Gentiles. They returned when the Russians liberated Warsaw. Instead of feeling happy that the war was over, they both felt a deep emptiness at all that had been lost. Not wanting to remain there, in a city where Meed had spent her entire life, the couple left Europe on May 24, 1945, on a boat to the United States. They married and settled in New York City where they still live today. They had two children who both grew up to be physicians.

It would be 1978 before Vladka and Benjamin Meed returned to visit Warsaw. They were shocked at the lack of recognition for the Jewish lives that were lost and at the deplorable state of the city's cemetery. Not wanting facts about this time in history to be forgotten, Vladka published her memoirs, *On Both Sides of the Wall,* in 1979. It has been published in Yiddish, Hebrew, Spanish, Japanese, and German, as well as English. In 1981, she and her husband established the Benjamin and Vladka Meed Registry of Jewish Holocaust Survivors so that survivors who had come to the United States could document their lives and locate relatives.

From her home in New York City, Meed writes articles, lectures internationally, and serves on boards and committees related to the

SS guards evacuate the Warsaw ghetto. Meed published her memoirs so that events like this would never be forgotten.

Holocaust. She has been a Yiddish-language radio commentator. She is currently a vice president with the Jewish Labor Committee, an organization with an early anti-Nazi history that works today to promote labor equity and social justice. The winner of numerous awards, Meed works with teachers to improve classroom instruction about the Holocaust and has produced a video on the Warsaw ghetto for use in education. She is the director of American Teachers Seminars on Holocaust and Jewish Resistance, which is run annually and includes a tour of the death camps in Poland.

When asked about heroism, Vladka Meed denies that she and others in the Warsaw ghetto were heroes. In her opinion, people like her mother were ordinary people simply attempting to live their lives, trying, despite the war, to maintain what they felt was important: families, school, the synagogue, and traditions. "Did they think about being heroes?" Meed asks rhetorically. "No, they were going on with [their] lives, the way they were used to, the way they believed." Meed insists, "I was not a heroine. I was not raised as such.

Meed shakes hands with President Jimmy Carter. Meed received many awards for her heroic acts during the Holocaust.

I don't see the big act. We were doing this as [a] normal way of living. This was the way we lived. This was our action and response for what the Germans were doing." [46]

However, Vladka Meed's own response *was* unique. She could have waited out the war disguised as a Gentile and escaped the dangerous missions she repeatedly chose to take. Her choice, made freely and with great courage, was to help her people live through the war.

CHAPTER 5

André Trocmé: "We Will Not Betray Them"

For Pastor André Trocmé, the phrase "love thy neighbor" had special significance. Anyone who came to the little French town of Le Chambon needing assistance received it. The French Protestant villagers opened their homes and farms to thousands of Jewish refugees and kept them hidden until the end of the war.

The charismatic Trocmé, often called the "living spirit" of the town, was imprisoned for defying the orders of the Nazi-controlled Vichy government and encouraging the sheltering of Jews. After his release, he went into hiding in order to keep his family and his parish safe. However, no amount of hardship could have forced him to compromise his belief that the only way to fight evil was to stand up for what was right.

Early Isolation

André Trocmé was raised in a world divided by war. He was born on Easter Day in 1901 in Saint-Quentin in northeast France. In his early childhood days, Trocmé witnessed firsthand the events of World War I when Saint-Quentin was occupied by the Germans. The spiritual convictions that would shape André's life were probably formed in his childhood.

André Trocmé grew up in a wealthy family with international roots. His father, Paul Eugene Trocmé, a lace manufacturer, came from a long line of French Protestants, or Huguenots. His mother, Paula Schwerdtmann, was German. These German roots set André apart from his Protestant neighbors, who were themselves a minority in the Catholic-dominated France.

The Trocmé family tended in other ways, as well, to be isolated in their community. The large home had a walled garden where André played with his brothers and sisters, apart from the neighborhood children. André did not go to school but was taught by private tutors. Paul Trocmé discouraged his family from mingling with the local people. He did not approve of the smoking and drinking of others, including the German relatives of André's mother. Despite his father's disapproval, André preferred his mother's side of the family, finding them warm and friendly.

"The Thing"

Several significant events occurred in André's youth that were to have an enormous impact on him later in life. The first of these, according to Trocmé biographer Phillip Hallie, author of *Lest Innocent Blood Be Shed: The Story of the Village of Le Chambon and How Goodness Happened There,* was the death of André's mother in 1911 in a car accident when the boy was almost ten. André's father was driving the car and was angry at another driver who had passed him. Despite pleas from the children and André's mother, Paul Trocmé refused to slow down. The two cars crashed and afterward André found his mother lying motionless on the road. André remembered his father screaming: "I killed her. I killed her." [47]

A rare 1943 photograph of André Trocmé playing the harmonica while imprisoned for disobeying Nazi orders.

She died three days later. André was profoundly affected by the sight of his mother's motionless body on the road, later referring to her body as "the thing." He struggled the rest of his life with the question of life after death, especially with the concept that one moment a person could be full of life and the next moment, all that could be lost and they could be "a thing." André also had to learn from this early experience, according to biographer Hallie, how to forgive.

The Union of Saint-Quentin

Another formative experience for the young André Trocmé was his membership in a group called the Union of Saint-Quentin. The Union of Saint-Quentin met to read, pray, and confess sins. Their meeting place was a simple room in the temple where they held their own services. For André, "this place and this group were paradise on earth" [48] because they offered him the spiritual community that was important to him his entire life.

This group did not ignore what was going on around them in Saint-Quentin. Defying the Germans, they secretly fed the Russian prisoners being held in German camps in Saint-Quentin in 1916. Years later, Trocmé remembered the importance of this community of people who put their goodness to work.

In 1917, when André was a teenager, his family fled to Belgium to escape the war. When he returned, toward the end of the fighting, their town, still occupied by Germans, had been transformed into a place of death, full of the wounded. Years later, Trocmé would recall the intense odors of the decaying bodies, and the trains that crossed through town en route to incinerators. The hatred of the French for

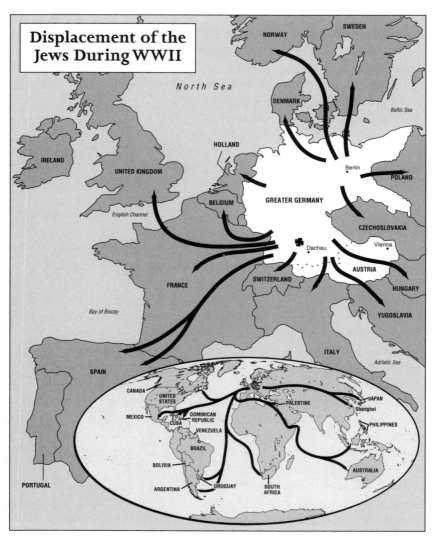

the Germans made a big impression on young André, and yet he did not share this hatred. He found it difficult to hate the injured young soldiers, particularly one German whose jaw had been blown off. Hallie writes, "All he could think of as he looked at the blinded, stumbling monster was, Look there, see what you have done to your brother." [49]

Around this same time, André was to meet someone who had another view of war, one that André himself would later embrace. One day, a young German soldier came to André's house and as they were speaking, the soldier explained to André that he was not an enemy, that no man was his enemy. The soldier, named Kindler, told him, "I shall not kill your brother; I shall kill no Frenchman. God has revealed to us that a Christian must not kill, ever. We never carry arms." [50] Intrigued with this alternative to the violence of war, André took Kindler to his union meeting. This German soldier was a conscientious objector, the first Trocmé would meet. Trocmé would not forget him.

The Study of Theology

After the war ended, Trocmé's family moved to Paris, where André studied theology at the University of Paris. Again, André sought out a group that would share his interest in prayer and community. He joined the Fellowship of Reconciliation, a pacifist group. He also continued with his involvement in unions, which were usually made up of the poor. As Hallie notes, Trocmé "stayed clear of the wealthy bourgeoisie among whom most of his relatives moved." [51]

André's studies in theology continued abroad. In 1925, André won a scholarship to Union Theological Seminary in New York City. It was here that he met Magda Grilli, a social worker who would become his wife. Magda, whose mother was Italian and whose father was Russian, had been brought up a Catholic, but she no longer practiced any particular religion or belonged to a church. Together, André and Magda returned to France. In the summer of 1926, they were married.

André and Magda Trocmé quickly began a family. Their daughter, Nelly, was born in the French town of Maubeuge. The next year, they moved to Sin-le-Noble, also in northern France, near Belgium, where three more children, Jean-Pierre, Jacques, and Daniel, were born. In 1934, the family moved to Le Chambon in southeast France.

Nonviolence in Le Chambon

Le Chambon-sur-Lignon was a town with distinctive characteristics. It was a mountain village, located high on a plateau and isolated

The quaint town of Le Chambon was a safe haven for Jews during the Holocaust.

from other towns. The winters were cold and long, lasting as much as nine months of the year. The three thousand villagers who lived there were independent and rugged. Many of them were Protestants who, like the Huguenots of André's family, had known a history of struggle and challenge in a country that was predominantly Catholic. Their isolation and their own history of persecution is said to account for the ease with which the residents of Le Chambon defied authority and listened instead to the advice of their pastors.

The Trocmés lived in the presbytery and brought to the peasants of this little town their experience as international travelers. André Trocmé was a passionate, charismatic man, full of energy in a town that was quiet for all but the three-month summer tourist season. The townspeople readily responded to such a leader. Magda Trocmé describes her husband's role in the town:

> The village of Le Chambon was a Protestant one, with a big church. On Sundays, the sermon was something very important, because at that time there was no movies, no special lectures. The sermon was something everyone wanted to hear. My husband's preaching was different because he was a conscien-

tious objector. The Protestant Church was not happy about it, because at that time conscientious objectors were not admitted as ministers. But the parish wanted a man like my husband, not only because of his ideas about war and peace but on account of his general ideas about truth and justice.[52]

André set up a school in Le Chambon, a place where children would prepare for their baccalaureates, as well as learn about non-violence and peace. To help run it, in 1938 he brought in Édouard Theis, a teacher and pacifist whom André had met in New York. This emphasis on nonviolence, both in Trocmé's church and the Cévenol School, was risky. Trocmé's insistence that the duty of Christians was to live a nonviolent life was in opposition to Hitler's war in Nazi Germany. But the townspeople supported Trocmé's philosophy. Eventually the school would house refugees from the war, as would other organizations in the town.

With the German occupation of France in June 1940, Trocmé's stance on nonviolence carried more risk. Le Chambon was located in the unoccupied territory of the country, the Free Zone, but the entire government was now controlled by the Germans. Trocmé knew that any acts of resistance against this government, the Vichy government, were serious, but he could not in good conscience offer his support. He continued to speak out against war and to perform other acts of defiance as well. For example, he refused to require his students to salute the French flag. He also would not sign an oath of allegiance to the chief of the French state. This resistance was only the beginning.

Refuge at Le Chambon

The town's role as a source of refuge developed slowly, beginning with a knock on the door. Magda describes the night it happened:

A poor woman came to my house one night, and she asked to come in. She said immediately that she was a German Jew, that she was running away, that she was hiding, that she wanted to have shelter. She thought that at the minister's house she would perhaps find someone who could understand her. And I said, "Come in." And so it started. I did not know that it would be dangerous. Nobody thought of that.[53]

Trocmé wanted to do more than shelter an occasional refugee. He wanted to volunteer in the camps, providing support for imprisoned Jews. In 1941, Trocmé met with a conscientious objector and Quaker named Burns Chalmers, who was working on liberating Jews. Magda Trocmé recalls Chalmers's response that what he needed was "a village, a house, a place to put people who are hiding, people that we can save." Chalmers told André, "We get people out of the camps, but nobody wants them. It is dangerous to take them. Is your village prepared to do such a thing?"[54]

The villagers were ready. Working quietly and asking few questions of the refugees, the townspeople, by the end of the war, had sheltered five thousand Jews. They hid them in barns and farm-

A group of Jewish survivors sits under a sign directing the way to Le Chambon. Many Jews survived by taking refuge in the small town.

houses, gave them false identity cards, brought them into the town's seven group homes, and later even accompanied them along dangerous escape routes into neutral Switzerland. Filmmaker Pierre Sauvage, himself one of those rescued, returned to Le Chambon to produce a documentary about the village. He calls what the Chambonnais did "a conspiracy of goodness." [55] Trocmé, as the village spiritual leader, was at the center of it.

Speaking Out Against Injustice

While the act of sheltering Jews was done quietly, without fanfare and without discussion among villagers, Trocmé did not try to hide his own acts of resistance. In the summer of 1942, when an official visited the town to recruit the village youth to government service, Trocmé handed him a paper on which he had clearly stated his opposition to the German treatment of the Jews in France. In the paper, Trocmé referred to a specific act of Nazi brutality, in which twenty-eight thousand Jews were rounded up in July 1942 and held without food or sanitation in the Paris arena, the Vélodrome d'Hiver, before being shipped off to German camps where they most likely died.

Trocmé was afraid that such actions might soon be applied to the Jews in the unoccupied zone that included Le Chambon. In his letter, Trocmé writes frankly of his position on the matter of sheltering Jews:

> We feel obliged to tell you that there are among us a certain number of Jews. But, we make no distinction between Jews and non-Jews. It is contrary to the Gospel teaching. . . . If our comrades, whose only fault is to be born in another religion, received the order to let themselves be deported, or even examined, they would disobey the orders received, and we would try to hide them as best we could. [56]

Trocmé's admission did not go unpunished. Two weeks later the chief of police came to the village and requested that Trocmé turn over the names of the hidden Jews. Trocmé refused. He was willing to tell them that the Jews were hidden in Le Chambon, but that was all. In fact, Trocmé and the villagers had been preparing for this moment, having arranged that in a time of danger such as this, the sheltered Jews would move from their farms into the surrounding woods. The buses that the Vichy police had brought to fill with Jews for deportation remained empty. The police stayed in Le Chambon for three weeks during the summer of 1942, but could find only one man to arrest. In fact, some of the police began to resist orders and were "converted" into helping the Chambonnais keep their refugees safely hidden.

From left to right André Trocmé, Roger Darcissac, and Édouard Theis celebrate their release from a Nazi internment camp.

The Imprisoned Pastor

This "conspiracy of goodness" was not without risk. On February 13, 1943, the French Vichy police arrested Pastor Trocmé. He and two other leaders, André's assistant pastor, Édouard Theis, and teacher Roger Darcissac, were taken to a Vichy detention camp near Limoges, a city northwest of Le Chambon. Their fellow inmates were political prisoners, mostly Communist leaders of the resistance. In camp, a strange thing happened. Trocmé and Theis began leading daily services that included Bible readings, hymns, and discussion about Christianity and communism. When the meeting tripled in attendance, the Vichy authorities sent in an officer to see what was going on. Using a code word for the French leader Marshal Petain, Trocmé was able to speak freely with the men about reasons to oppose this anti-Semitic government now in place. Hallie observes, "The camp was becoming an organized group of resisters against Vichy right under the eyes of Vichy." [57]

After a month in prison, the three men were released, even though Trocmé and Theis stayed true to their beliefs and refused to sign an oath of allegiance to the Vichy government. The prison director told them that someone powerful had ordered it, but later no one could determine who that was, or why. However, it was fortunate for Trocmé and Theis that they did leave the camp because days later the remaining inmates were sent to concentration camps, where most of them died.

Trocmé Goes into Hiding

By the summer of 1943, Le Chambon had become a dangerous place. Trocmé's cousin, Daniel Trocmé, and his house of refugee children were taken away to the death camp Majdanek in eastern Poland. (Daniel Trocmé was killed at the camp on April 4, 1944.) Germans were putting pressure on resisters, and Trocmé was told that because he was a target for assassination, it would be best for the town if he went into hiding. Trocmé was reluctant to do this but was finally convinced that it was best for the town. He carried a forged identification card, shaved off his mustache, and put on glasses. He moved from place to place, occasionally visited by members of his family. After the Allies landed in Normandy in June 1944, Trocmé returned to the village after a year's absence.

The Death of a Son

Later that summer, on August 13, 1944, Trocmé and his wife were to suffer the terrible loss of their eldest son, Jean-Pierre. The young teenager was found hanging from a pipe in the bathroom of their home. It was never known whether his death was an intentional suicide or an accident. The doctor who examined him guessed that Jean-Pierre had been imitating a staged hanging he had observed the evening before at a reading of the poem "The Ballad of the Hanged." André Trocmé was deeply affected by his son's death. In his notes, André would write that even thirty years later, "I carry a death within myself, the death of my son, and I am like a decapitated pine. Pine trees do not generate their tops. They stay twisted, crippled." [58] (Another son, Daniel, would be killed in a car accident in 1962 in the United States.)

Daniel Trocmé, André's cousin, also endeavored to hide Jews, but was discovered and executed in 1944.

Lectures on Nonviolence

Despite the devastating loss of his son, Trocmé continued in his work. As the war was coming to a close, Trocmé encouraged members of his parish not to engage in the attacks against the Germans that were occurring elsewhere in France. Biographer Hallie notes that Trocmé continued to preach to both his parishioners and German prisoners "sermons based upon the ten Commandments and upon the belief that Christ had shown us that we must forgive sins instead of killing the sinner." [59]

The town was liberated in September 1944. The refugees left and the town returned to its quiet state before the war. After a few years André Trocmé began to travel around Europe and the United States, lecturing on nonviolence for the Fellowship of Reconciliation, an interfaith organization that promotes peace.

Later, he served as a pastor in Geneva, where he remained until his death in 1971 of a stroke. He was cremated and was buried in Le Chambon, next to the graves of his sons. Pastor Édouard Theis delivered a sermon on June 12, 1971, one that Trocmé had written just hours before his death.

Trocmé's Legacy

André Trocmé and his wife, Magda, were chosen as "Righteous Among the Nations" by the Yad Vashem in 1971. It was an honor that would have pleased him, although perhaps he would not have thought that simple human kindness to one's neighbor warranted an award. Survivor André Couraqui offered the Yad Vashem this testimony:

> Pastor André Trocmé was the living soul and the spiritual personification of the French resistance. Through his personal actions, as an example to others by his demands and by his writings, Pastor André Trocmé undoubtedly saved—directly and indirectly—numerous Jewish souls, and helped to strengthen the spirit of the French resistance which, at the end of the day, contributed to the downfall of the National Socialism of Hitler. Pastor Trocmé always offered me the most complete and reliable assistance. No month went by when I did not turn to him for help; to him or to his friends or to the members of his congregation who were hiding Jews in that area. During all the tragic years of our resistance, Pastor Trocmé always answered our calls for help. He answered them with enthusiasm, even though he

Jewish survivors stand before a school in Le Chambon. Residents hid Jews in homes and schools during the Holocaust.

knew his efforts on our behalf endangered his life, those of his wife and children, and those of his congregation. His church and his home were among the great centres of the French resistance. [60]

When Pierre Sauvage returned to Le Chambon to make his film, he interviewed many people who remembered Trocmé and who could speak for the spirit of this small village. One of them, Leslie Maber, spoke of the choices the people of her village were faced with.

Humanity is fundamentally good with the possibility to become fundamentally bad. And there's [a] choice. It doesn't mean that bad people are all bad, and good people are all good. It doesn't mean that in Le Chambon there are no people with faults and failings. It's a community like any other community. I think that means that any community anywhere has the choice to make and can choose right. And the people who seem very ordinary people can do great things if they're given the opportunity. [61]

Le Chambon was given the opportunity. With the encouragement and guidance of spiritual leader André Trocmé, the townspeople did a great thing in offering refuge to thousands of people who could not find it elsewhere.

CHAPTER 6

Hannah Senesh: Poet, Parachutist, Partisan

In times of peace, Hannah Senesh might have grown up to be a poet, a playwright, or a teacher. These were the personal interests she put to the side when, at eighteen, she left Hungary in pursuit of a Jewish homeland in Palestine (now Israel). As much as she loved her native country, she was convinced that the only way the Jewish people could live a life free of prejudice was to establish a country of their own. In Palestine, she joined other hardworking young people who were studying agriculture and learning how to be self-sufficient on this desert land.

After four years in Palestine, Hannah made a courageous decision. She decided to leave the peace and safety of Palestine and return to Hungary to rescue her mother and to participate in the resistance to the Nazis. She joined the British forces and parachuted behind enemy lines, where she joined partisan fighters. After crossing the border into Hungary, she was captured by the Germans and imprisoned. On November 7, 1944, at the age of twenty-three, she was executed by firing squad. Although she lived a short life, Hannah Senesh is remembered for being a source of inspiration and hope to those in the throes of a terrible war.

Early Years in Budapest

Hannah Senesh was born on July 17, 1921, into a Jewish family of privilege in Budapest, Hungary, a city where, historically, there had been little anti-Jewish sentiment. Hannah's early years were happy ones, spent with her parents, Catherine and Bela, her grandmother whom they called "Fini Mama," and her brother, George. Her father, Bela Senesh, was a well-known writer. He had a column in the newspaper and his plays were popular in the Budapest theater.

Despite Hannah's later interest in Zionism, her family was not particularly religious while she was growing up. The Seneshes, biographer Anthony Masters notes, "were a very good example of integrated Jews." [62] They attended the synagogue on holidays and celebrated the Sabbath on Friday evenings, but they were very much a part of the musical and cultural world of Budapest, including the theater. Like other assimilated Jews, Bela Senesh had changed his name—from Schlesinger to the less Jewish-sounding Senesh. Bela and Catherine's social and professional friends included both Christians and Jews.

Hannah's father was in poor health in her early years, having a heart condition brought on by childhood rheumatic fever. He spent as much time with his children as he could, taking them on outings, telling them stories, and bringing them into his bedroom so that they could sit on the end of his bed while he rested. He died of a heart attack in May 1927 when Hannah was five. It was a loss that would

Hannah Senesh, seated in her garden, worked behind enemy lines as part of the resistance.

stay with Hannah throughout her brief life, and she mentions him often in her diary. Hannah's childhood was punctuated with visits to the cemetery. "I can hardly remember Daddy (his face)," she writes in 1935 in the journal that she would keep until shortly before her own death, "but just the same I love him very much, and always feel he is with me." [63]

A Popular Student

Hannah was a good student, though she struggled with French. She attended a Protestant high school that enrolled both Christian and Jewish students. With a mother's affection, Catherine Senesh remembers her daughter as "considerate, gentle, conscientious, responsible." [64] Hannah was a friendly child who tutored other students for a couple hours each week in order to earn a little extra money for skating and dancing lessons. With her green eyes, wavy brown hair, and friendly smile, Hannah had an engaging personality that drew people to her.

Hannah wrote often in her journal, using it to record her thoughts as she grew from a child into a young adult. In it, she recorded descriptions of trips she took, activities, friends, and, as she grew older, her confusion over her relationships with boys, many of whom showed more interest in her than she did in them. On many occasions, she used her journal to contemplate what her role in life would be. In August 1936, she writes, "I still long to be a writer. It's my constant wish. . . . And I would like to be a great soul. If God will permit!" [65] Her literary talents were evident in the many poems she wrote throughout her life. On at least two occasions she had her poetry read by professional writers who offered her suggestions and encouragement. Hannah also wrote plays and performed them at home or shared them with her classes at school.

Growing Tensions in Budapest

At a young age, Hannah was aware, as all Jews were, of the effect her Judaism would have on the course of her life. In 1937, when she was sixteen, she was nominated as secretary at her school's literary society, but not allowed to hold the office because she was Jewish. In 1938, and then again in 1939, anti-Jewish laws were passed in Hungary and rights were restricted. Hungary's Jews had reason to be fearful, particularly in light of the continuing Nazi threat in neighboring countries.

Hannah's diary reflects her sensitivity to the increasingly dangerous climate in Hungary. She was aware of the mounting anti-Semitism, and the growing presence of the Arrow Cross, a Fascist

Officials view the slain bodies of Jews on the streets of Budapest, the city where Hannah Senesh spent her childhood.

organization that would later commit vicious acts against the Jewish people in Budapest. Hannah writes about the "terrible tension" in Hungary after Nazi troops occupied Austria and then Czechoslovakia in 1938. She declares in her journal that she is prepared for the worst that might come, but, of course, she was not. "No one was prepared," observes biographer Masters, "and no one had any conception of what the worst was to be." [66] Hungary was to lose half of its eight hundred thousand Jews before the war ended. When Hannah's brother's plans to study in Austria were no longer possible and he decided instead to study textiles in France at the University of Lyons, Hannah and her mother were glad he would be safely out of Hungary.

"I've Become a Zionist"

The increase in anti-Semitism in Hungary—and Hannah's growing pride in being a Jew—preceded her declared commitment to Zionism in the fall of 1938. On October 27, 1938, she abruptly announced in her journal that she had become a Zionist. "One needs something to believe in," she states in a 1938 entry, "something for which one can have whole-hearted enthusiasm. One needs to feel that one's life has meaning, that one is needed in the world. Zionism fulfills all of this for me." [67]

This belief that hope for the Jewish people lay in Zionism, a separate Jewish homeland free from persecution, consumed Hannah. She began to study Hebrew and to prepare to emigrate to Palestine where she planned to live on a kibbutz, a collective farm where she would learn farming skills. In a paper she read at a Bible meeting in 1939, she made this declaration:

Members of a kibbutz pose at the entrance to their farm. Senesh hoped to live on a similar farm.

One of the fundamentals of Zionism is the realization that anti-Semitism is an illness which can neither be fought against with words, nor cured with superficial treatment. . . . We don't want charity. We want only our lawful property and rights, and our freedom, for which we have struggled with our own labours. It is our human and national duty to demand these rights. We want to create a Homeland for the Jewish spirit and the Jewish people. The solution seems so very clear: we need a Jewish State. [68]

Her Mother's Resistance

Hannah's mother, Catherine, resisted the idea of Hannah's immigration to Palestine. Catherine was convinced that conditions would improve and that Hannah should abandon this idealistic notion to be a pioneer in a land so far from home. Catherine wanted Hannah to remain in Budapest, a city where Jews had assimilated, until life could return to normal after the war.

Hannah Senesh would not give up her plan to go to Palestine, insisting to her mother that she could not be happy if she remained in Hungary. Finally, she departed on September 13, 1939, just ten days after World War II was declared. The departure was difficult for both mother and daughter. Still enroute, eighteen-year-old Hannah wrote home: "Truly, Mother dear, that moment when the train started and I could not control myself, was extremely difficult. Regardless of the fact I was so overjoyed about the journey, I forgot all my dreams, plans, and hopes, and at that moment felt only the pain of parting with you for a very long time." [69] It would be five years before Hannah saw her mother again.

Learning to Farm

In Palestine, Senesh began her studies at the Nahalal Agricultural School, which offered rigorous training in the science of agriculture. The school was founded with the belief that both men and women needed to be prepared equally for work on the land in order for Palestine to succeed agriculturally. For two years, she lived and worked at the school, adjusting to the dry, hot desert and the physical labor of farming. She took classes, tended to the cows and chickens, picked fruit, and baked bread.

In her journal and sometimes in letters, she would write of her decision to live there. She wondered if she had made the right decision to leave her mother behind. She wondered if she could be doing something better than working on the land. Ultimately, however, she decided that she loved being in Palestine for the lack of prejudice, and for what she called "the knowledge that the smallest matters are not decided by the criterion of whether one is a Jew or not." [70]

When her agricultural education was complete in 1941, she moved to a kibbutz, a small community of young people working together on a collective farm, where the living conditions were quite primitive. Increasingly her diary reflects her growing sense of frustration at being so far from Europe where the war was raging and where Hungary struggled to remain neutral.

By January 1943, she was obsessed with thoughts of her mother's safety in Budapest and her brother in France, with whom she had lost contact for some time. She did not know it, but her brother had fled German-occupied France that December. "I can think of nothing now but my mother and brother. I am sometimes overwhelmed by dreadful fears. Will we ever meet again?" [71] She searched for a way to make this happen but travel through occupied Europe was dangerous. Few routes led safely into Hungary and immigration out of the country was difficult too.

A Dangerous Mission

When Senesh heard of a parachute mission that was being formed, she was immediately convinced that this was the way to get back to her homeland and her mother. The mission required that she join the British army and be dropped behind enemy lines. The plan was for her to join partisans on the ground and work with them to gather information about German activities. A primary goal was to help downed Allied pilots make their way out of enemy territory so that they could return to the air. Senesh also hoped to return to Budapest and bring her mother out of the country and, eventually, to the safety of Palestine. Not realizing that this mission was doomed to fail, Hannah eagerly signed up with a handful of other young, inexperienced, idealistic people.

Her preparation began in Haifa, a coastal city in northern Palestine, where she entered basic training in the summer of 1943. The first stage of her training was ideological: she learned about the causes behind the Holocaust, as well as the ideals of Judaism and Zionism, so that she could communicate this to those she came into contact with. The second part of the training came later that year and included drills in military maneuvers and weaponry. She was taught to work as part of a team and how to survive in the countryside if left on her own. Later, in early 1944, she continued her training in Cairo, Egypt, where she was taught Morse code and how to parachute safely.

Before she left for Egypt, she was surprised to discover that her brother, George, had finally reached Palestine, where he, too, had chosen to join the Zionist movement. They met for one final emotional reunion. She kept the details of her mission a secret, showing him only a letter in which she had written, "There are times when one is commanded to do something, even at the price of one's life." [72] Then she was gone. Her final entry in her diary, written January 11, 1944, conveys her last-minute trepidation and her reluctance to share it: "This week I leave for Egypt. I'm a soldier. Concerning the circumstances of my enlistment, and my feelings in connection with

George Senesh, pictured with Hannah, also joined the Zionist movement.

Jewish parachutists pose with women from the Yugoslavian underground. Senesh parachuted into Yugoslavia in 1944.

it, and all that led up to it, I don't want to write. I want to believe that what I've done, and will do, are right. Time will tell the rest." [73]

On the Ground in Yugoslavia

Finally, the day came for the mission to start. To Senesh's profound disappointment, the mission was changed at the last minute. The small band of parachutists, only a half dozen of them, would land in Yugoslavia, not Hungary, which was now occupied by the Germans. Fellow parachutist Reuven Dafne remembers Hannah Senesh as being fearless on the way to the jump. She was also the only one who was certain that the mission would succeed. "Never once did she consider the possibility of failure; never once did she allow us to become dispirited or discouraged." [74] Dafne recalls that Senesh would, like the rest of them, have periods of discouragement, but that her optimism always renewed itself and she was able to lift the spirits of her comrades.

On the ground in Yugoslavia, the Jewish Mission marched for months, working with the partisans on intelligence gathering and sabotage as they blew up trains and captured small patrols of Germans. One of the stated aims of the Jewish Mission was to communicate hope to those Jews on the ground, to let fellow Jews know that there were forces among them engaged in active resistance.

The Young British Officer

Hannah Senesh was an inspiration to those she met. Parachutist Yoel Palgi remembers marching for up to two days at a time without stopping, enduring rain and wet ground, enemy fire, hunger, and fatigue. "Hannah was unmistakenly our leader. She was the only woman who had ever parachuted into Yugoslavia from a friendly country, and she knew how to talk to a general as well as a private." [75]

Dafne remembers that Senesh captivated the people in her British officer uniform, with her pistol at her side. People had heard about her in advance. In fact, she had become something of a legend, not because she was a woman—many partisan fighters were women—but because, according to Dafne, of a "special, mysterious quality" that "excited their wonder and respect." [76]

Senesh still endeavored to write poetry during this time. Inspired by the spirit of one of the women partisans she met, Senesh wrote the poem "Blessed is the Match," which is recited by Israeli schoolchildren today. Days before she crossed the Hungarian border, she wrote this poem and gave it to one of her comrades, who crumpled it up and tossed it away, and then returned the next day to recover it.

Capture in Hungary

After three months in Yugoslavia, Senesh was eager to cross into Hungary to rescue her mother and other Jews in danger there. However, Hungary was now in the throes of a war it had hoped to avoid. Under the command of Adolf Eichmann, the Nazis worked feverishly in the spring of 1944 to deport great numbers of Hungary's Jews to the death camp of Auschwitz. Crossing into Hungary at this time was extremely dangerous. Senesh's comrades would not chance it.

Palgi recalls Senesh's stubborn insistence that they make the attempt. As always, she was relentless about standing up to the Germans, despite the risk. She told him, "We are the only ones who can possibly help, we don't have the right to think of our own safety; we don't have the right to hesitate. Even if the chances of our success are minuscule, we must go." [77] Senesh believed this, but her comrades felt the crossing was too dangerous and refused to accompany her. Hannah lashed out in anger toward anyone who did not see it her way.

Finally, with several partisans, Senesh made the decision to go. In the final moments before Senesh left, Dafne recalls her good spirits. "She was bubbling with joy, forthright, impish, and amazingly carefree. She seemed to be like someone about to embark upon an experience she had been looking forward to for years." [78] That was the last time Dafne saw her. She crossed into Hungary on June 9, 1944, and was almost immediately captured.

Imprisoned in Budapest

Although she had attempted to discard her radio transmitter and guns, this incriminating evidence was quickly found. She was beaten and interrogated by the Germans, but she would not talk. She was moved to a prison in Budapest where her mother was brought in to persuade Hannah to give up the secret codes that the military police wanted to use to infiltrate the partisans. Hannah broke down completely at the sight of her mother. Of Hannah's appearance, her mother later would write: "Had I not known she was coming, perhaps in that first moment I would not have recognized the Hannah of five years ago. Her once soft, wavy hair hung in a filthy tangle, her ravaged face reflected untold suffering, her large, expressive eyes were blackened, and there were ugly welts on her cheeks and neck." [79]

To persuade Hannah to talk, her mother was also imprisoned. Through various methods, the two were able to communicate. Messengers conveyed notes. Hannah spoke with the guards in their own language and gained their sympathy. Prison matrons allowed Catherine Senesh to send a birthday gift to her daughter on her twenty-third birthday. Hannah was able to pass her mother writings. When Hannah was in solitary confinement, she placed her table on her bed, a chair on top of it, and climbed up to send communications through the high windows. Using letters she cut out, she spoke to other inmates, including her mother.

Senesh earned a reputation for being fearless and informed. She picked up information through newspapers and through speaking with other prisoners on her frequent trips in police vans. She shared what she had learned about Hitler's activities and the advancement of Russian troops. She spoke, too, about Zionism.

In September, both Hannah and her mother were moved to different jails. Then her mother was freed and immediately went to work on her daughter's release. Hannah's trial was to be held on October 28, 1944. The charge against her was treason. She was accused of joining the British forces, crossing the Hungarian border illegally, and having a radio transmitter in her possession.

She pled not guilty. Then she made a statement in which she explained, at length, how much she loved her country and how it was the "conscienceless leaders," the "traitorous generals of German sympathies who reigned in Hungary" [80] who were guilty of treason to the thousands of Hungarians who had died.

Her sentence was not immediately decided. She was told it would take eight days. With the war coming to an end, Senesh believed that whatever her sentence might be, it would be shortened when the Germans were defeated.

Senesh's Death

However, in a most tragic turn of events, Hannah Senesh's sentence was not to be time in prison. She was given the supreme penalty for treason—death. On November 7, 1944, she was allowed one hour to prepare for her death. She was not allowed to say any good-byes. Her mother was to discover her death after it had occurred.

The young Zionist was taken into the prison yard and positioned in front of a firing squad. In her final moments, she was defiant. Refusing a blindfold, Hannah looked at her executioners directly and calmly as they raised their guns and shot her.

When word got around the prison that a young British parachutist had been executed, the other prisoners were

Yoel Palgi stood at attention for over an hour after hearing of Senesh's execution.

shocked. No one could believe it had happened. Out of respect, some of the prisoners, including her comrade Yoel Palgi, stood at attention for over an hour.

Afterward her mother was given a letter that Hannah wrote in that last hour. Her final words to her mother were "Dearest Mother, I don't know what to say—only this; a million thanks, and forgive me, if you can. You know so well why words aren't necessary. With love forever, your daughter." [81]

A Hero in Israel

Senesh was initially buried in Budapest, but in 1950 her remains were moved to Israel and given a hero's burial in a military cemetery. Her plays have been performed and several of her poems have been made into songs. Her diary and letters have been published in several languages. Recognized as a national hero, Senesh has become the subject of plays and a movie. A village, Yad Hannah, is named after her.

Hannah Senesh is seen as a symbol of courage, determination, and selfless sacrifice. Her worldview is reflected in these words from her diary: "We have need of one thing: people who are brave and without prejudices, who are not robots, who want to think for themselves and not accept outmoded ideas."[82] Senesh was not a robot. She died thinking for herself, inspiring others, and speaking out through her actions and her poetry for what she felt would help the Jewish people in Hungary and Palestine.

CHAPTER 7

Jan Karski: If Only They Would Listen

Jan Karski's career as a diplomat to his country, Poland, had just begun when war broke out in 1939. From that point on, Karski's service to his country would take a form he would never have imagined for himself. As a courier for the Polish underground, the refined, peaceful Karski found himself crossing Nazi-held Europe to deliver messages to the Polish government-in-exile in France. He was caught and tortured, but after a daring escape, he continued with the dangerous mission of delivering the truth to the Allied leaders in Britain and the United States.

He had witnessed firsthand what was happening to the Jewish people in the Warsaw ghetto and death camps and was eager to convey this vital information to Allied leaders. Despite his reports that the Jews were being exterminated, nothing was done in response. He was remembered until his death in 2000 as the man who tried to tell the world what was really happening during World War II.

Jan Karski used his position in the Polish government to aid Jews in Poland.

A Formative Childhood in Lodz

Jan Karski was born Jan Kozielewski in Lodz, Poland, on April 24, 1914. His mother was a sensitive woman, a devout Roman Catholic, and the mother of eight children. She taught her children the importance of religious tolerance in a city where a large percentage of the population was Jewish. Karski, an obedient child who took his mother's teachings to heart, was the youngest. Two siblings died before Karski was an adolescent. His father died when Jan was young, so he "didn't register much in his heart and mind," [83] Karski later admitted. His eldest brother, Marian, older by eighteen years and active in the Polish underground, became like a father to him.

Karski displayed a devotion to Catholicism at a young age. Enrolled in a Jesuit elementary school and strongly influenced by the Jesuit fathers there, twelve-year-old Karski joined a group of fellow students who studied morality and the Bible under the mentorship of a Jesuit priest. Karski would have an abiding loyalty to the Jesuits, an order of the Roman Catholic Church, his entire life. Karski would later explain, "As a child I was taught an individual has human dignity, responsibility to society, to our Lord." [84]

Encouraged by his politically minded older brother Marian, Karski knew he wanted to be a diplomat before he had completed high school. He was an exceptional student, relying on his excellent memory, a skill that would serve him well later. A formative experience in his teenage years was his friendship with some Jewish students at his gymnasium, or what Americans call a prep school. Karski and this small group of Jewish students studied together, they helping him with his physics, chemistry, and algebra, and he helping them with their history, literature, and poetry.

A Young Patriot

In college, Karski pursued his ambition to be a diplomat or an ambassador. A profession in which he communicated with other countries on behalf of Poland was greatly appealing to him. He enjoyed studying international diplomacy and relations and was deeply patriotic. He was so fascinated by the concept of a life spent in diplomatic service that he wrote his college thesis on Talleyrand, Napoléon's foreign minister. Years later Karski would talk about how he labored over this project in which he attempted to reconstruct every day of Talleyrand's life. In 1935, Karski graduated from Jan Kazimierz University in Lwøw, earning two master's degrees, one in law, the other in diplomatic science.

Karski spent a year after graduation serving in the military. He distinguished himself at equestrian and military technique. Afterward, in 1936, he began his career in diplomacy, traveling to Geneva, Switzerland, to work under the Polish foreign ministry with an international labor organization. A year later, the foreign ministry transferred him to London to work in the Polish embassy there. This gave him an opportunity to learn English. In late 1938, he returned to Warsaw and was admitted into a training program for foreign ser-

German and Soviet military officers sign an agreement to divide Poland.

vice. Having earned very high marks, in January 1939 he was given his first important position with the foreign ministry. His diplomatic career was advancing quickly.

However, his career plans were disrupted when Poland was invaded that summer by both Russian and German troops. On August 23, Karski was called back into active duty as an officer. In a country split between Russian and German control after the German–Soviet nonaggression pact, Karski was captured by the Russians in territory once held by Poland. With other military officers, Karski was thrown into a Russian prisoner of war (POW) camp. After weeks in captivity, Karski managed to escape by disguising himself as a foot soldier and volunteering to be part of a prisoner trade with the German POW camp. *En route,* Karski was able to convince a half-dozen other prisoners to join him in jumping from the train. The guards fired repeatedly, but the train continued on and Karski was uninjured. He walked back to Warsaw. He was most fortunate to have left the Russian POW camp when he did. Many of his fellow prisoners were taken to Russia and died in harsh labor camps or were executed there.

First Mission for the Polish Underground

In Warsaw, Karski was to make the decision that would affect his activities throughout the war. There, he contacted his brother Marian, who was a police chief, now under command of the Germans. Along with other Poles who had an allegiance to Poland, Marian was secretly committed to the exiled government of General Wladyslaw Sikorski, located in France. Although it was very dangerous, Jan Karski joined this underground movement. Like the other underground groups in existence in Poland, this one was prepared to fight the Germans in case of an uprising. A large part of underground activity was devoted to secretly gathering information to use against the Germans, as well as maintaining contacts with the exiled Polish government.

Karski was assigned his first mission: to communicate with the government-in-exile in France. Karski was chosen because of his intelligence and his special memory skills. He also had experience traveling outside of Poland. He later stated that the underground leaders "knew I knew Europe. I knew languages. So they used me as a courier." [85]

Before he proceeded on the trip to France, his brother sent him on official police business. Using police documents, he was to travel throughout Poland, gathering information about the changes the Germans had wrought. He also was instructed by his brother to get word

German soldiers force a Jewish man to cut his beard. Karski observed this type of public humiliation in his travels throughout Poland.

to the police forces across Poland, directing them to stay on their jobs so that they could maintain a stronger position against the Germans.

While traveling around Poland, Karski was dismayed to learn of the low morale of the defeated country and realized that with the Nazis in power, the Jews of Poland were in grave danger. Karski saw how the Gestapo regularly taunted and abused Jews on the street, calling them names, tossing cold water on them in freezing weather, and stealing from their streetside stands with no respect for them as people.

His First Mission

When Karski returned to Warsaw, he prepared to embark on his first courier assignment for the underground. He had the task of delivering a report on conditions in Poland to General Sikorski, now positioned in France. In early 1940, Karski began an adventurous trip across Europe through enemy territory. The trip, for which he had a well-paid mountain guide who was in the business of smuggling people, required that Karski ski across the newly formed Slovakia to get to Hungary. When he reached Budapest, he rested there to nurse his blistered feet before continuing on through Yugoslavia, Italy, and France, using false papers and traveling first-class by train. He met with Polish officials in southwest France, exchanged information about the current situation in Poland, and delivered a message from his brother, who wished for guidance on how to best serve as police chief under Nazi rule, and for advice on how to operate other underground activities. In April, Karski, armed with information committed to memory, made the return trip, traveling the same route but on foot, as the snow had now melted.

When Jan Karski arrived in Warsaw, he discovered that his brother Marian had been seized by the Gestapo on police conspiracy charges. (Marian would be sent to Auschwitz but was later released.) Jan soon established other contacts in the underground and was able to communicate the information he had carried back with him from France.

A Failed Mission

His next mission was directed by the Political Coordinating Committee, a group made up of leaders of various underground groups. Despite some contention, these groups were determined to work together, using Karski to carry information from each leader to the government-in-exile in France. After meeting with each leader individually, Karski set out on the same route, this time making a crucial error in judgment. *En route* to France, Karski let an important underground leader in Kraków persuade him to carry along a roll of film that held pictures of important underground documents. This put Karski in more danger. Ordinarily he carried nothing and committed everything to memory.

Karski, usually a very careful man, was to make a second mistake, as well. Feeling that his mission was urgent, Karski ignored the advice of his guide, who wished to delay the trip a few days until a fellow guide returned from a previous crossing. Karski's guide feared that something had gone wrong. Karski was impatient and insisted they proceed. The two of them walked part of the route to avoid the Gestapo troops in the area. After days of hiking, Karski was exhausted and they were forced to stop for the night at a peasant hut. In the middle of the night, Karski woke to the pain of a policeman's rifle pounding into the side of his head. Quickly, Karski tossed the incriminating film into a bucket of water by the stove, hoping that the Gestapo would not find it. Then he was carted off to jail, where he would discover that the Germans had intercepted other couriers at this peasant hut. Karski's guide had been right to want to delay the passing.

His biographers describe Karski's fears as he waited to be interrogated: "He lay on a straw pallet in a tiny cell, wiping the blood from his face and wondering what would come next. Tales of Gestapo torture had already taken on legendary proportions within the underground. There could be no doubt that the Germans would use any means available to extract information from him, nor would they place any value on his life once he was no longer of use to them." [86]

Tortured by the Gestapo

Unfortunately, the film was discovered by the police and Karski could offer no credible explanation for what was on it. He was considered a spy. His fears were realized as he was interrogated repeatedly and beaten badly in the face and head each time he refused to provide information. His ribs were broken and several of his teeth were knocked out. Unable to stand the torture and knowing that he could not reveal the truth of his mission, he decided to take his own life. He cut his wrists with a razor blade he had hidden in his boots.

Fortunately he did not die, but woke up instead in a hospital where the Slovak doctors encouraged him to appear sicker than he was so that he could stay there. Eventually, he was sent back to a hospital in Poland where Jozef Cyrankiewicz, a prominent member of the Polish underground, helped arrange a daring escape in which his rescuers sedated the guards, helped Karski scale a fence, and then fled in a rowboat across a wide river to reach a hiding place in a barn. All his life, Karski remained grateful to Cyrankiewicz, who later be-

Guards beat a Jewish prisoner at a labor camp. Karski experienced similar brutality while incarcerated.

came the Communist prime minister of Poland. Those who had aided him at the hospital were not so lucky. Some—even those not involved in the escape—were tortured. And some were killed. None would reveal Karski's whereabouts.

After months of hiding, Karski returned to Warsaw and worked in low-profile tasks for the underground, listening to the radio and attempting to stay informed of the Nazis' plans for Warsaw and the rest of the region. With his scarred wrists, Karski was in constant danger of discovery, but that did not keep him from embracing a new mission, an assignment that would be his biggest yet.

A Visit to the Ghetto and Death Camp

In the summer of 1942, the Polish underground needed a courier who could travel to London to meet with Allied leaders. Karski was eager to serve. He would be carrying messages from resistance groups all over Warsaw, including the Jewish resistance. Jewish leader Leon Feiner insisted that Karski relay a list of demands, including a request for funds. With money, a properly placed bribe could buy food, medicine, or false documents that could save a life. Here is Feiner's poignant plea, as recounted in *Karski: How One Man Tried to Stop the Holocaust*: "You Poles are also suffering. . . . But after the war, Poland will be restored. Your wounds will slowly heal. By then, however, Polish Jewry will no longer exist. Hitler will lose this war, but he will win the war he has declared against the Polish Jews." [87]

According to Feiner, there was no power in Poland that could help the masses of Jews now facing imminent destruction. Neither the Polish nor the Jewish underground movements could offer more than marginal assistance. Therefore, the responsibility for at least making some effort to help lay with the governments of the nations allied against Germany. "Let not a single leader of the United Nations be able to say that they did not know that we were being murdered in Poland and could not be helped except from the outside," [88] declared the Bund leader. History, he added, would hold them responsible if they failed to act.

A poor man walks the streets of a Polish ghetto. Karski sought to inform people all over the world of the horrors that Jews faced during the Holocaust.

Karski would not be the first to report on what was happening to Europe's Jews. Feiner had made earlier attempts to inform Jewish and Allied leaders. To be more convincing and to "present more tangible evidence," Feiner suggested that Karski witness the "Nazi extermination machine in operation." [89] Karski agreed.

Nothing could have prepared Karski for what he saw in the Warsaw ghetto. Dressed as a poor Jew, he entered the ghetto. There, he saw firsthand the horrid conditions that the Jewish people were forced to endure. He describes the scene in his *Story of a Secret State:*

> A cemetery? No, for these bodies were still moving, were indeed often violently agitated. These were still living people, if you could call them such. For apart from their skin, eyes, and voice there was nothing human left in these palpitating figures. Everywhere there was hunger, misery, the atrocious stench of decomposing bodies, the pitiful moans of dying children, the desperate cries and gasps of a people struggling for life against impossible odds.[90]

At the death camp, he saw only death. He watched in horror as prisoners were shoved and packed in train boxcars and then burned to death as the quicklime the Nazis had spread on the car floors ate into the victims' skin and lungs and asphyxiated them.

Later in his life, Karski would decline to talk of what he had seen. "I saw terrible things, things in Poland, particularly concerning the Jews that I don't want to remember today. I want to keep my sanity." [91]

Speaking with World Leaders

As he traveled to England, Karski carried with him the memory of these horrific images, along with a tiny roll of film, so small that it could fit into a hollowed key. He arrived in London in November 1942 and met with Polish, Jewish, and British officials, including the British foreign minister Anthony Eden, who told him that Britain had already done all it could do by accepting one hundred thousand refugees. Before the meeting, Karski had admired Eden. "For me he was the epitome of the career government official—competent, dignified, intelligent," Karski was to say later. "But my opinion changed when I found him very abrupt and unwilling to discuss the problem of the Jews in Poland." [92] Karski was pleased though that his visit did have influence in the press as articles began appearing and demonstrations were held.

Karski continued with his mission, this time in the United States. On July 28, 1943, he met with President Franklin Roosevelt, who declined to give money, insisting that currency for bribes would be a way

Karski attempted to convince President Franklin Roosevelt to save Poland's Jews.

of subsidizing Hitler. Roosevelt also insisted that the best way to help the Jews would be to win the war. According to Karski, the president said, "Justice, freedom will prevail. You will tell your nation that they have a friend in this house. This is what you will tell them."[93]

When Karski returned to London at the end of August, he was told by Polish officials that it was too dangerous for him to return to Poland. After some discussion about what to do with him, Polish officials decided to send him back to the United States. This time he was free to speak openly about what was going on in Poland. During this trip, Karski had more meetings, this time with prominent religious leaders, journalists, and political figures. Karski also wrote prolifically, publishing articles in magazines and newspapers and delivering two hundred lectures all over the United States. His book *Story of a Secret State* appeared at the end of 1944 and was a book-of-the-month selection and a best-seller. In it were key chapters detailing what he had seen in the Warsaw ghetto and the death camp.

A Political Exile and a New Career

When the war ended, Poland was run by a Communist regime that Karski was deeply opposed to and he became a political exile. He stayed in the United States on an entry visa until he was eligible to become a citizen in 1954. He worked as a lecturer, and met his wife, a Polish Jew whose family had died in the Holocaust. Deciding to continue pursuing foreign affairs, he earned a Ph.D. from the School of Foreign Service at Georgetown University, a Jesuit school, and was brought onto the faculty. He remained at Georgetown University, in Washington, D.C., for over four decades as a popular professor of international relations until he retired in 1984. In 1985, after fifteen years spent working on it, he published a highly regarded book called *The Great Powers and Poland, 1919–1945*.

For many years after the war, Jan Karski did not speak of his past. His first interview after decades of silence was with filmmaker Claude Lanzmann, who convinced Karski to tell his story on camera for his documentary *Shoah*. After this, Karski began to speak of what he had seen and done in the war.

A Life Devoted to Peace

Karski's experiences with war made him seek a life of peace. He came to believe later that it is individuals who make choices, who have souls—not governments. "I reported to the most powerful leaders," he said. "There were leaders of the government, of the nations. They discarded their personal opinions, which might have been sympathetic towards Jews." [94]

He also came to realize the awful power of war: "War degrades people because war generates hatred, you have to hate. People, individuals, who otherwise would not do such things, when they have war,

Karski in his office at Georgetown University. Karski devoted his life to fighting religious intolerance and anti-Semitism.

when they fight, they will do unimaginable things. Derail a train—never mind that innocent people will be killed. Throw a grenade—never mind that children will be killed. . . . And this I never realized before this hatred."[95]

Karski chose to live a life without hate. He stayed committed to his mission of diplomacy, throughout the war and long after as he worked to educate and shape young minds in the classroom. In a foreword to a book on Holocaust survivors, Karski writes eloquently of his hope for the world: "We have an infinite capacity to do good and an infinite capacity to do evil. It is up to every one of us to make a choice. Our Lord endowed us with a free will. Let us then oppose and combat religious intolerance, fanaticism, anti-Semitism, and racism. They are sinful. They are also stupid. They stand in the way of progress."[96]

Recognition as a Hero

Jan Karski received numerous awards in his lifetime. These included honorary degrees from American universities and Warsaw University, and various awards bestowed by Jewish, Polish, Catholic, and nondenominational groups, as well. Karski traveled throughout the United States, and went to Israel in 1982 to accept an award as a "Righteous Gentile." In 1994, President Lech Walesa made him a Knight of the White Eagle, the highest honor in Poland. This same year he was also made an honorary citizen of Israel, which he considered a great honor.

Jan Karski died at the age of eighty-six on July 13, 2000. He was remembered in obituaries across the world as a hero who tried to stop the war.

NOTES

Introduction: The Importance of Heroes

1. Carol Rittner and Sandra Myers, eds., *The Courage to Care: Rescuers of Jews During the Holocaust*. New York: New York University Press, 1986, p. xv.

2. Quoted in Rittner and Myers, *The Courage to Care*, p. x.

Chapter 2: Oskar Schindler: A Kind Nazi

3. Emilie Schindler with Erika Rosenberg, *Where Light and Shadow Meet: A Memoir*. New York: W. W. Norton, 1996, p. 28.

4. Schindler, *Where Light and Shadow Meet*, p. 27.

5. *Oral History Interview with Ludmilla Page*, dir. by Sandra Bradley. March 11, 1992, videocassette.

6. Quoted in Thomas Fensch, ed., *Oskar Schindler and His List*. Forest Dale, VT: Paul S. Eriksson, 1995, p. 25.

7. Quoted in Eric Silver, *The Book of the Just: The Unsung Heroes Who Rescued Jews from Hitler*. New York: Grove Press, 1992, p. 149.

8. Quoted in Fensch, *Oskar Schindler and His List*, p. 29.

9. *Oral History Interview with Leopold Page*, dir. by Sandra Bradley. March 11, 1992, videocassette.

10. *Oral History Interview with Ludmilla Page*.

11. Quoted in Elinor J. Brecher, *Schindler's Legacy: True Stories of the List Survivors*. New York: Penguin, 1994, p. 70.

12. Quoted in Fensch, *Oskar Schindler and His List*, p. 18.

13. *Oral History Interview with Leopold Page*.

14. Quoted in Fensch, *Oskar Schindler and His List*, p. 19.

15. Quoted in Mordecai Paldiel, *The Path of the Righteous: Gentile Rescuers of Jews During the Holocaust*. Hoboken, NJ: KTAV Publishing, 1993, pp. 168–69.

Chapter 3: Raoul Wallenberg: A Man with a Mission

16. Raoul Wallenberg, *Letters and Dispatches, 1924–1944*, trans. Kjersti Board. New York: Arcade Publishing, 1995, p. 31.

17. Harvey Rosenfeld, *Raoul Wallenberg: Angel of Rescue*. Buffalo, NY: Prometheus Books, 1982, p. 17.

18. Quoted in Rosenfeld, *Raoul Wallenberg*, p. 19.

19. Wallenberg, *Letters and Dispatches*, p. 171.

20. Rosenfeld, *Raoul Wallenberg*, p. 23.

21. Wallenberg, *Letters and Dispatches*, p. 221.

22. John Bierman, *Righteous Gentile: The Story of Raoul Wallenberg, Missing Hero of the Holocaust*. Rev. ed. London: Penguin Books, 1995, p. 50.

23. Elenore Lester, *Wallenberg: The Man in the Iron Web*. Englewood Cliffs, NJ: Prentice-Hall, 1982, p. 163.

24. Wallenberg, *Letters and Dispatches*, p. 230.

25. Quoted in Rosenfeld, *Raoul Wallenberg*, p. 51.

26. Quoted in Rosenfeld, *Raoul Wallenberg*, p. 58.

27. Rosenfeld, *Raoul Wallenberg*, p. 68.

Chapter 4: Vladka Meed: Between Two Worlds

28. *Oral History Interview with Vladka Meed*, dir. by Linda Kuzmack. June 19, 1991, videocassette.

29. *Oral History Interview with Vladka Meed.*

30. *Oral History Interview with Vladka Meed.*

31. Vladka Meed, *On Both Sides of the Wall: Memoirs from the Warsaw Ghetto*. New York: Holocaust Library, 1979, p. 12.

32. Meed, *On Both Sides of the Wall*, p. 40.

33. Meed, *On Both Sides of the Wall*, p. 54.

34. *Oral History Interview with Vladka Meed.*

35. Meed, *On Both Sides of the Wall*, p. 79.

36. Meed, *On Both Sides of the Wall*, p. 85.

37. Meed, *On Both Sides of the Wall*, p. 85.

38. Meed, *On Both Sides of the Wall*, p. 85.

39. Meed, *On Both Sides of the Wall*, p. 110.

40. Meed, *On Both Sides of the Wall*, pp. 129–30.

41. *Oral History Interview with Vladka Meed.*

42. Meed, *On Both Sides of the Wall*, p. 133.

43. Meed, *On Both Sides of the Wall*, p. 147.

44. *Oral History Interview with Vladka Meed.*

45. Meed, *On Both Sides of the Wall*, p. 172.

46. *Oral History Interview with Vladka Meed.*

Chapter 5: André Trocmé: "We Will Not Betray Them"

47. Phillip Hallie, *Lest Innocent Blood Be Shed: The Story of the Village of Le Chambon and How Goodness Happened There.* New York: Harper and Row, 1979, p. 52.

48. Hallie, *Lest Innocent Blood Be Shed*, p. 55.

49. Hallie, *Lest Innocent Blood Be Shed*, p. 58.

50. Hallie, *Lest Innocent Blood Be Shed*, p. 59.

51. Hallie, *Lest Innocent Blood Be Shed*, pp. 61–62.

52. Rittner and Myers, *The Courage to Care*, p. 100.

53. Rittner and Myers, *The Courage to Care*, pp. 101–2.

54. Rittner and Myers, *The Courage to Care*, p. 103.

55. *Weapons of the Spirit*, prod. and dir. by Pierre Sauvage. First Run Icarus Films, 1987, videocassette.

56. Hallie, *Lest Innocent Blood Be Shed*, p. 102.

57. Hallie, *Lest Innocent Blood Be Shed*, p. 38.

58. Hallie, *Lest Innocent Blood Be Shed*, pp. 258–59.

59. Hallie, *Lest Innocent Blood Be Shed*, p. 261.

60. Silver, *The Book of the Just*, p. 21.

61. *Weapons of the Spirit.*

Chapter 6: Hannah Senesh: Poet, Parachutist, Partisan

62. Anthony Masters, *The Summer That Bled: The Biography of Hannah Senesh.* London: Michael Joseph, 1972, p. 22.

63. Marta Cohn, trans., *Hannah Senesh: Her Life and Diary.* New York: Schocken Books, 1972, p. 19.

64. Cohn, *Hannah Senesh*, p. 8.

65. Cohn, *Hannah Senesh*, p. 25.

66. Masters, *The Summer That Bled*, p. 38.

67. Cohn, *Hannah Senesh*, p. 63.

68. Cohn, *Hannah Senesh*, pp. 69–70.

69. Cohn, *Hannah Senesh*, p. 79.

70. Cohn, *Hannah Senesh*, p. 146.

71. Cohn, *Hannah Senesh*, p. 126.

72. Cohn, *Hannah Senesh*, p. 132.

73. Cohn, *Hannah Senesh*, p. 131.

74. Cohn, *Hannah Senesh,* p. 172.

75. Cohn, *Hannah Senesh,* p. 185.

76. Cohn, *Hannah Senesh,* p. 174.

77. Cohn, *Hannah Senesh,* p. 186.

78. Cohn, *Hannah Senesh,* p. 178.

79. Cohn, *Hannah Senesh,* p. 207.

80. Masters, *The Summer That Bled,* p. 287.

81. Cohn, *Hannah Senesh,* p. 242.

82. Cohn, *Hannah Senesh,* p. 133.

Chapter 7: Jan Karski: If Only They Would Listen

83. *Oral History Interview with Jan Karski,* dir. by Gay Block and Malka Drucker. February 22, 1988, videocassette.

84. Gay Block and Malka Drucker, *Rescuers: Portraits of Moral Courage in the Holocaust.* New York: Holmes & Meier Publishers, 1992, p. 172.

85. *Oral History Interview with Jan Karski.*

86. Thomas E. Wood and Stanley M. Jankowski, *Karski: How One Man Tried to Stop the Holocaust.* New York: John Wiley & Sons, 1994, p. 74.

87. Wood and Jankowski, *Karski: How One Man Tried,* p. 118.

88. Wood and Jankowski, *Karski: How One Man Tried,* p. 118.

89. Wood and Jankowski, *Karski: How One Man Tried,* p. 120.

90. Jan Karski, *Story of a Secret State.* Boston: Houghton Mifflin, 1944, p. 330.

91. *Oral History Interview with Jan Karski.*

92. Quoted in Harry James Cargas, *Voices from the Holocaust.* Lexington: University Press of Kentucky, 1993, p. 62.

93. Quoted in Cargas, *Voices from the Holocaust,* p. 63.

94. *Oral History Interview with Jan Karski.*

95. *Oral History Interview with Jan Karski.*

96. Nick Del Calzo, *The Triumphant Spirit: Portraits & Stories of Holocaust Survivors . . . Their Messages of Hope & Compassion.* Denver, CO: Triumphant Spirit Publishers, 1997, p. 10.

FOR FURTHER READING

Books

Linda Atkinson, *In Kindling Flame: The Story of Hannah Senesh, 1921–1944*. New York: Beech Tree Books, 1985. Hannah Senesh's life story, with many passages from her journals and letters.

Deborah Bachrach, *The Resistance*. San Diego: Lucent Books, 1998. Covers the various forces of resistance during the Holocaust, including the ghettos, the partisans, and the actions of a defiant Denmark. Also includes a chapter on the early refusal of the United States to offer aid.

Miriam Chaikin, *A Nightmare in History: The Holocaust, 1933–1945*. New York: Clarion Books, 1987. The events of the Holocaust, with an emphasis on the stories of the victims. Personal accounts, diary excerpts, and photos are used to illustrate.

Milton Meltzer, *Never to Forget: The Jews of the Holocaust*. New York: HarperCollins, 1976. Comprehensive, readable summary of the Holocaust.

————, *Rescue: The Story of How Gentiles Saved Jews in the Holocaust*. New York: Harper and Row, 1988. Very readable chapters devoted to various Gentiles and their heroic endeavors.

Jack L. Roberts, *The Importance of Oskar Schindler*. San Diego: Lucent Books, 1996. An informative biography of Schindler, with photos. Told in the context of the war in Poland and Czechoslovakia.

Seymour Rossel, *The Holocaust: The War and the Jews, 1933–1945*. Springfield, NJ: Behrman House, 1992. Overview of the Holocaust, with well-selected graphics and photos; discussion questions on key issues covered.

Linda Schmittroth and Mary Kay Rosteck, eds., *People of the Holocaust*, vols. 1 and 2. Detroit: U.X.L., 1998. Profiles of sixty key figures in the Holocaust, in two volumes, with informative sidebars. Includes victims, Nazis, and world leaders who played a part.

Victoria Sherrow, *The Righteous Gentiles*. San Diego: Lucent Books, 1998. The stories of those Gentiles who chose to help the Jews. Organized by country.

WORKS CONSULTED

John Bierman, *Righteous Gentile: The Story of Raoul Wallenberg, Missing Hero of the Holocaust*. London: Penguin Books, 1995. The story of Wallenberg and his disappearance.

Gay Block and Malka Drucker, *Rescuers: Portraits of Moral Courage in the Holocaust*. New York: Holmes & Meier Publishers, 1992. Profiles, with photos, of brave participants of the Holocaust, organized by country.

Elinor J. Brecher, *Schindler's Legacy: True Stories of the List Survivors*. New York: Penguin, 1994. Riveting stories told by survivors of the Holocaust.

Harry James Cargas, *Voices from the Holocaust*. Lexington: University Press of Kentucky, 1993. Interviews with Holocaust figures, including Jan Karski.

Marta Cohn, trans., *Hannah Senesh: Her Life and Diary*. New York: Schocken Books, 1972. A superb collection of Hannah Senesh's diaries, letters, poetry, as well as essays from her mother and others close to her in her final days.

Lucy S. Dawidowicz, *The War Against the Jews, 1933–1945*. New York: Holt, Rinehart & Winston, 1975. A definitive history of the Holocaust, including a summary of the main events that occurred in each country during the war.

Nick Del Calzo, *The Triumphant Spirit: Portraits & Stories of Holocaust Survivors . . . Their Messages of Hope of Compassion*. Denver, CO: Triumphant Spirit Publications, 1997. The personal stories of ninety-two Holocaust survivors, with a foreword by Jan Karski and an introduction by *Schindler's List* author Thomas Keneally.

Thomas Fensch, ed., *Oskar Schindler and His List: The Man, the Book, the Film, the Holocaust and Its Survivors*. Forest Dale, VT: Paul S. Eriksson, Publisher, 1995. A collection of articles about Schindler, including Herbert Steinhouse's noteworthy "The Man Who Saved a Thousand Lives."

Martin Gilbert, *Never Again: A History of the Holocaust*. New York: Universe Publishing, 2000. An overview of the Holocaust, with well-selected archival photos, maps, and documents.

Phillip Hallie, *Lest Innocent Blood Be Shed: The Story of the Village of Chambon and How Goodness Happened There*. New York: Harper and Row, 1979. Philosopher Hallie tells the story of André Trocmé and Le Chambon, with an emphasis on ethics.

Peter Hay, *Ordinary Heroes: The Life and Death of Chana Szenes, Israel's National Heroine*. New York: Paragon House, 1989. A detailed narrative of the life of Hannah Senesh.

Jan Karski, *Story of a Secret State*. Boston: Houghton Mifflin, 1944. Out of print, but still available in some libraries, this book was written to make the world more aware of the atrocities of Hitler.

Thomas Keneally, *Schindler's List*. New York: Simon & Schuster, 1982. This story of Oskar Schindler, written in narrative form, is a detailed biography of Schindler. Steven Spielberg based his movie *Schindler's List* on this book.

Elenore Lester, *Wallenberg: The Man in the Iron Web*. Englewood Cliffs, NJ: Prentice-Hall, 1982. The story of Raoul Wallenberg's life, set against the background of Hungary in 1944.

Anthony Masters, *The Summer That Bled: The Biography of Hannah Senesh*. London: Michael Joseph, 1972. The story of Hannah Senesh is interwoven with the events of the war in Hungary.

Vladka Meed, *On Both Sides of the Wall: Memoirs from the Warsaw Ghetto*. New York: Holocaust Library, 1979. Meed's personal account of life in the Warsaw ghetto and the resistance movement.

Mordecai Paldiel, *The Path of the Righteous: Gentile Rescuers of Jews During the Holocaust*. Hoboken, NJ: KTAV Publishing, 1993. The stories of many rescuers, organized by country. A thorough presentation of the impact of the Holocaust on each country and the variety of approaches used to thwart the Nazis.

Carol Rittner and Sandra Myers, eds., *The Courage to Care: Rescuers of Jews During the Holocaust*. New York: New York University Press, 1986. Profiles of rescuers and reflective essays about the courage required to save lives.

Harvey Rosenfeld, *Raoul Wallenberg: Angel of Rescue*. Buffalo, NY: Prometheus Books, 1982. A well-documented story of Raoul Wallenberg and his disappearance.

Emilie Schindler with Erika Rosenberg, *Where Light and Shadow Meet: A Memoir*. New York: W.W. Norton, 1996. Emilie Schindler tells her own story about her life with Oskar Schindler.

Eric Silver, *The Book of the Just: The Unsung Heroes Who Rescued Jews from Hitler*. New York: Grove Press, 1992. The stories of those heroes, both recognized and unknown, who made sacrifices to help the Jews. Includes diplomats, the clergy, prisoners, and entire communities who rescued Jews.

Raoul Wallenberg, *Letters and Dispatches, 1924–1944*, trans. Kjersti Board. New York: Arcade Publishing, 1995. Personal letters between Wallenberg and family are included here, as well as Wallenberg's reports from Budapest.

Thomas E. Wood and Stanley M. Jankowski, *Karski: How One Man Tried to Stop the Holocaust*. New York: John Wiley & Sons, 1994. A compelling, thorough account of Karski's endeavors in Europe and the United States.

Documentaries and Oral History Interviews

Oral History Interview with Jan Karski. Dir. by Gay Block and Malka Drucker. February 22, 1988, videocassette. Karski speaks from his home about his activities during the Holocaust, including his analysis as a diplomat of how this could have happened to the Jewish people.

Oral History Interview with Leopold Page. Dir. by Sandra Bradley. March 11, 1992, videocassette. Leopold Page talks about his memories of Oskar Schindler, including the liberation of the Jews in the Brinnlitz factory.

Oral History Interview with Ludmilla Page. Dir. by Sandra Bradley. March 11, 1992, videocassette. Ludmilla Page talks about life in the ghetto and her personal memories of Oskar Schindler.

Oral History Interview with Vladka Meed. Dir. by Linda Kuzmack, June 19, 1991, videocassette. In this extensive interview, Vladka Meed talks about her life in Warsaw, her comrades in the underground, and her thoughts on heroism.

Schindler. Dir. by Jon Blair. Thames International, 1995, videocassette. This documentary tells the story of Schindler's life, relying on interviews with people who were saved.

The Warsaw Ghetto. Prod. by Hugh Burnett. Dir. by James Colina. With narrator, adviser, Alexander Bernfes. BBC-TV, 1967, videocassette. Narration accompanies actual footage taken by Nazi videographers. Graphic and disturbing footage.

Weapons of the Spirit. Prod. and dir. by Pierre Sauvage. First Run Icarus Films, 1987, videocassette. Sauvage returns to the village of Le Chambon where he and his parents were sheltered and interviews inhabitants to tell the story of the remarkable town.

Websites

All three of these sites provide an extensive collection of Holocaust material and links to other sites.

Jewish Virtual Library (www.us-israel.org). An encyclopedia of articles related to the Holocaust, including timelines, biographies, photos, maps, and a glossary.

Simon Wiesenthal Museum of Tolerance, Multimedia Learning Center (http://motlc.wiesenthal.com). A comprehensive collection of resources, including photos, articles, exhibits, and "Frequently Asked Questions" about the Holocaust.

United States Holocaust Memorial Museum (www.ushmm.org). The museum's "Holocaust Learning Center" is easy to use and provides an excellent overview of the Holocaust, including personal stories and photos.

INDEX

PICTURE CREDITS

ABOUT THE AUTHOR

Susan Glick has written many articles about places to go and things to do with children in the Washington, D.C., area. In spring 2003, her first work of fiction, a story for young adults called *One Shot,* will be published by Henry Holt. Ms. Glick, who has a master's degree in English language and literature from the University of Maryland, has also taught writing to students of all levels, from elementary school to college. Currently she works with high school students who have learning disabilities. Ms. Glick lives in Silver Spring, Maryland.